CW00848184

ABC GUIDE 1

HUMAN LIFESPAN DEVELOPMENT

Level 3

Mark Walsh

textbook
training

Published by Textbook Training *Publishers*
Learning support for health and social care

© Text copyright Mark Walsh 2016

Mark Walsh asserts the moral right to be identified as the author of this work.

Also available in this series:

Working in Health and Social Care – An ABC Guide for Students
ISBN 978 - 1533500151

Anatomy and Physiology – An ABC Guide for Students
ISBN 978 - 1533500182

Meeting Individual Care and Support Needs – An ABC Guide for Students
ISBN 978 - 1533500229

Psychological Perspectives – An ABC Guide for Students
ISBN 978 - 1533499790

Sociological Perspectives – An ABC Guide for Students
ISBN 978 - 1533500274

Introduction

This *ABC Guide to Human Lifespan Development* covers XX entries that define, discuss and explain a range of concepts, terms and theories that feature in the human development units of level 3 health and social care courses. These include *Unit 1 Human Lifespan Development* of the *BTEC National Health and Social Care* course, *Unit 4 Development through the Life Stages* of the *OCR Level 3 Cambridge Technical Health and Social Care* awards as well as some of the human development content in *GCE AS / AS Health and Social Care and Psychology* courses. The *ABC Guide to Human Development* has been written to provide learners with a broad ranging resource to support learning within these particular units.

Unlike a textbook, this book is not designed to be read sequentially. You can find and access information about any one entry as the need arises but also follow some links between entries to build up and develop your understanding of a topic area. Try using a particular term as a 'way in' or jumping off point and go from there!

At the end of each entry the *See also* suggestions are used to indicate how the term is connected to other issues, debates and topics within and beyond the unit you are studying. You are encouraged to follow up some of these links and to move between the entries to clarify and deepen your understanding. References are also provided where appropriate and could be followed up as a way of extending your knowledge and understanding if you have a strong interest in a particular topic or issue.

I hope that you find the material in the *ABC Guide* helpful in your studying.

Mark Walsh

Activity theory

Activity theory, also known as the normal theory of ageing, proposes that people who cope with ageing best are those who stay active and maintain their network of social and family relationships.

The basic claim of activity theory is that the more active a person is in later adulthood, the more satisfied they will feel with their life. Activity theory developed in the 1960s as a way of countering social disengagement theory, an alternative and more negative view of ageing. Where disengagement theory suggests that older people do withdraw from, or are sometimes forced to give up, long-held life roles (as a worker, colleague or partner) because of 'old age', activity theory suggests people adapt to the effects of ageing most successfully, and live more satisfied lives, when they stay active.

Fennell, Phillipson and Evers (1989), for example, argue that older people often resist disengaging with the roles, relationships and activities that have been an important part of their lives and personal identities by maintaining a 'middle-age' lifestyle. This might involve taking part in social and educational activities as a way of staying physically and mentally healthy, for example. 'Keeping busy' with hobbies, friendships and social activities are, according to activity theory, important ways of avoiding stagnation and the loss of mental and physical skills (summed up in the phrase 'use it or lose it').

Critics of activity theory point out that not all older people can, or want, to 'keep busy'. Activity theory also doesn't seem to account for inequalities, diversity and difference in the older population. Instead, older people are assumed to be largely similar in their motivations, circumstances and abilities. In reality, some older people do lack the money, motivation and good health to maintain an active lifestyle whilst others don't see 'keeping busy' or taking on new challenges as a positive lifestyle choice in old age.

See also – Ageing process; Social disengagement theory

Reference
Fennell,G., Phillipson, C., and Evers, H. (1989), *The Sociology of Old Age*, Milton Keynes, Open University Press.

textbook
training

Adolescence

Adolescence is the third life stage, following on from childhood and before that, infancy.

Your course specification suggests that adolescence occurs between 9 and 18 years of age. It can be defined as a period of rapid, major physical growth and psychological development that generally occurs from the onset of puberty to the beginning of adulthood. The developmental changes that happen during this life stage are captured in the Latin origins of the term - 'adolescere' – which mean 'to grow up'.

In contrast to the relative lack, and slower pace, of physical change in late childhood, adolescence is seen as a very active, transitional stage of human development. This is largely because adolescence more or less coincides with puberty when physical changes to the body, particularly the development of primary and secondary sexual characteristics, lead to sexual maturity. As a result, girls' and boys' physical size and capabilities change markedly during adolescence. However, puberty can also begin before adolescence (especially in girls), and physical growth as well as psychological development that is not the result of puberty, can continue into a person's early twenties.

Adolescence has been studied by psychologists, sociologists, educationalists and historians, as well as biologists who focus on physical and physiological changes. Typically, it is seen as a period in which a person prepares, and is prepared, for the adult roles and relationships they will take on.

At the same time, psychologists argue that a person's cognitive or thinking skills change significantly during adolescence as they develop abstract thinking abilities. This is the ability to think hypothetically and about objects and issues that are not physically present.

The point at which adolescence begins and ends varies across societies and cultures. The end of adolescence is often marked by a person being granted new legal rights – such as the right to drive, vote or have sexual relationships, for example. At the same time, people tend to become more independent of their families, less accepting of adult authority and become responsible for making their own lifestyle decisions as they move out of adolescence and into the adult life stage.

See also – Life stage; Maturity; Peer pressure; Puberty; Hormones

Reference
O'Brien, E.Z. (2016), *Psychology for Social Work*, Palgrave Macmillan

Ageing process

The ageing process is a phrase used to describe the pattern of human physical change that occurs as people get older. More broadly, the ageing process involves physical, psychological and social changes throughout the human lifespan.

Humans experience a continuous process of physical, psychological and social development and change from birth until the end of life. Despite the fact that the ageing process has a lifelong, ongoing effect on human development, it is also often associated with physical and psychological *decline* rather than with development. This tends to occur because a distinction can be made between the process of 'maturation' (which occurs between birth and adulthood) and 'ageing' (which occurs from adulthood until the end of a person's life). From early adulthood onwards, the ageing process affects the way we change physically as well as our cognitive (intellectual) and psychological functioning.

The effects of the human ageing process are much more noticeable in middle adulthood, typically between the ages of 40 and 65, than in the early part of this life stage. People who are aged 40 are at about the midpoint of their life expectancy and will be aware of some loss of physical ability. For example, they may be aware that they run and walk more slowly than they did as young adults and may feel that they have less strength and stamina too.

Figure 1 - Physical changes experienced in adulthood

Physical function	Age of change	Nature of change
Vision	40 - 45	Thickening of the lens of the eye leads to poorer vision and more sensitivity to glare.
Hearing	Approx 50	Loss of ability to hear very high and very low sounds.
Muscles	Approx 50	Loss of muscle tissue especially fibres used for bursts of strength and speed.
Bones	After menopause in women, later in men	Loss of calcium in ones and wear and tear on the joints.
Heart and lungs	35 – 40	Decline in most aspects of function when measured during or after exercise but not at rest.
Reproductive system	Mid-30s for women	Increased risk of reproductive problems and lowered fertility.
Skin elasticity	Approx 40	Increase in wrinkles due to loss of elasticity

See also – Dementia; Life expectancy; Menopause;

Attachment

Attachment refers to the behaviour and emotions that occur in situations where a child experiences stress, fear or senses danger. Children show attachment behaviour by seeking closeness and protection from another (usually a parent or caregiver) who is seen by them to be stronger, wiser and a source of safety.

Attachment is a significant aspect of a child's development. John Bowlby (1951, 1953, 1958) introduced the concept into UK psychology and child care practice generally. He argued that attachment behaviour is a specific biological response resulting from a desire to seek security and protection from harm through physical and emotional closeness to an attachment figure. Bowlby's (1958) view is rooted in evolutionary psychology and the desire for self-preservation. Attachment is widely seen as normal and healthy behaviour and only becomes a source of concern when a child seems unable to function without an attachment figure when there is no obvious danger or source of stress present.

An infant's early emotional development plays an important part in their future relationships with others. Ideally, an infant should have opportunities to develop feelings of trust and security during the early years of life. Attachment behaviour tends to first develop at around 6 – 7 months old (Aldgate and Jones, 2006) and typically involves an infant developing a strong emotional link with her parents or main caregivers. The parent or carer response to this emotional linking is known as bonding. It is through attachment and bonding that an infant's first emotional relationship is formed.

An infant's response to the presence of others changes as they develop socially and emotionally:

- up to 6 months, anyone can hold the baby. The baby may protest when put down by whoever is holding them. This is known as indiscriminate attachment.
- between 7 and 12 months the baby's attachment behaviour is more evident and she is likely to show greater fear of strangers. This can be intense for 3 or 4 months and is known as specific attachment.
- from 12 months onwards the baby's attachments broaden to include other close relatives and people whom they see frequently. This is known as multiple attachment.

Attachment is often associated with infant and early childhood behaviours. However, attachments can be formed at any life stage and can persist over time (Howe, 1995). Attachment figures can be parents, care-givers or other significant adults in a person's life. The main criteria is that an attachment figure is seen as safe and protective. A child (or an adolescent or adult) can have good attachments to a number of care-givers or people with whom they have developed a safe, secure relationship.

Aldgate and Gibson (2015) suggest that attachment is linked to two behavioural systems. These are known as the exploratory behavioural system and the fear behavioural system. When a child feels unsafe, their attachment behavioural system is inactive. As a result, the child will feel safe and calm and be able to explore the world around them. However, in circumstances where they feel afraid and unsafe, their attachment behaviour is activated and their exploratory behaviour suppressed. The aim of attachment behaviour in these circumstances is to return the child to a state of equilibrium where they feel safe and calm. Seeking protection and security from the attachment figure enables this to happen.

It is thought that a person's early experience of attachment provides a 'blueprint' for subsequent relationships. Poor or faulty attachment, or problems with parental bonding, may lead to feelings of insecurity and difficulties in forming and maintaining trusting relationships later in life.

See also – Infancy; Emotional development; Social development

References
Bowlby, J. (1951), *Maternal Care and Maternal Health: WHO monograph Series No.2*. Geneva: World Health Organisation.
Bowlby, J. (1953), *Child Care and the Growth of Love*, Harmondsworth, Penguin.
Bowlby, J. (1958), 'The nature of the child's tie to its mother', *International Journal of Psycho-Analysis 39*, 350-353
Aldgate, J. and Jones, D. (2006), 'The Place of Attachment in Children's Development', In J. Aldgate, D. Jones, W.Rose and C.Jeffery (eds), *The Developing World of the Child*, Jessica Kingsley Publishing
Howe, D. (1995), *Attachment Theory for Social Work Practice*, Basingstoke: Macmillan
Aldgate, J. and Gibson, N. (2915), 'The Place of Attachment Theory in Social Work with Children and Families', in J. Lishman (ed) *Handbook for Practice Learning in Social Work and Social Care*, Jessica Kingsley Publishing

Bandura's theory

Albert Bandura (b. 1925) is the psychologist responsible for developing some of the main principles of social learning theory. He recognised that behaviourism could only explain how people learn directly through experience. People, and other animals, also learn *indirectly* by observing and imitating the behaviour of others. As a result, this perspective focuses on the effects that other people, such as parents, teachers, friends, peer group members, celebrities, sports performers and pop stars, for example, can have on an individual's development and behaviour. In particular, Bandura's social learning theory argues that some behaviour is acquired or learnt through imitation of admired people or role models.

Bandura et al (1961) carried out an experimental study involving 36 boys and 36 girls, all 4 years of age. In the experiment, the children were divided into three groups (12 boys and 12 girls in each group) carefully matched for aggression levels. The three groups were:

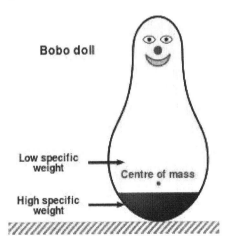

Figure 2 – An illustration of a Bobo doll

1. An aggressive model group who saw an adult being physically and verbally abusive to a Bobo doll (see diagram).
2. A non-aggressive model group who saw an adult act neutrally towards a Bobo doll.
3. A third control group didn't see an adult playing with the Bobo doll at all.

All of the children spent time in a room with toys they weren't allowed to play with. They were then put in a room with a Bobo doll. Bandura et al (1963) found that the children who were part of the groups that saw an adult being verbally and physically aggressive towards the bobo doll were more likely to treat the doll aggressively themselves than those children who saw the bobo doll being treated well or didn't see an adult playing with the doll at all. Bandura's famous 'Bobo Doll' experiment was used to develop and provide evidence for some of the principles of social learning theory.

Bandura (1961) argued that the bobo doll experiments showed that we learn through a process of imitating role models but that we only imitate those behaviours we see as being in our interests. Social learning theorists like Bandura say that for behaviour to be imitated it must be rewarded or reinforced in some way. This can occur through 'vicarious reinforcement' where an individual experiences indirect reinforcement by seeing their role model being reinforced. For example, a child may see their favourite footballer get away with a foul, score a goal and then get lots of praise from team mates and supporters.

As a result, they may decide to copy this aspect of their admired role model's behaviour the next time they play football themselves.

The social learning theory approach suggests that learning, and the development of behaviour, sometimes occurs with the need for direct reinforcement. Admired people (role models) are able to influence an individual's behaviour and identity if the individual is motivated to be more like their role model. People are motivated to be more like their role models if they admire or desire the personal attributes or qualities associated with them.

See also – Social factors; Parenting style; Peer pressure

Reference
Bandura, A. and Walters, R.H. (1963), Social Learning and Personality Development, New York: Holt, Rinehart and Winston

---

textbook training

Biological factors

Biological factors are biologically-based influences that affect the structure and functioning of the human body.

Examples of biological factors include the genes a person inherits from their parents, infections that they acquire, a person's diet, exposure to drugs or alcohol or any congenital defects they are born with. Biological factors may affect a person's development in the womb (e.g mother drinking excess alcohol leading to foetal alcohol syndrome) or after they have been born (e.g developing a hearing impairment following bacterial meningitis infection).

Primary, normal growth and development depends on (and is promoted by) biological factors such as genes, adequate diet and sufficient exercise. On the other hand, normal patterns of growth and development can also be disrupted or negatively affected by inherited genetic defects, excessive or poor quality diets, exposure to alcohol or other substances and inadequate levels of exercise.

See also – Brittle bone disease; Genetic factors

Brittle bone disease

Brittle bone disease (Osteogenesis imperfecta or OI) is a genetically acquired condition characterised by bones that fracture easily and frequently, often for no obvious reason (such as a fall or traumatic impact).

The underlying reason for the brittle bones people with OI have is a collagen disorder. Collagen is a protein that supports the mineral structure of the bones. Insufficient or poor quality collagen results in weak, fragile bones that fracture easily and unexpectedly. The Brittle Bone Society estimate that 1 in every 15,000 people will have this condition. There are a range of types of OI condition. The general characteristics of each are outlined in table 00 below.

Figure 3 - Types of Osteogenesis Imperfecta

Type of OI condition	Main features
Type 1 The milder and most common variant, often 'invisible' to the casual observer.	Children with this condition may be clumsy with hypermobile joints, are more likely to have falls and trip, are likely to become tired more easily, and may also have brittle / crumbling teeth. A child with Type 1 OI may require surgery and short-term use of a wheelchair for mobility problems. Adults – Often appear to be in

	good physical health but still at risk of fractures. Mobility and movement may be affected by effects of fractures sustained when younger. Can experience hearing problems.
Type II Severe and often life-limiting variant. Babies with this condition often die within a few months.	Often poor lung development due to problems with rib bones and subsequent breathing difficulties.
Type III A severe but not life-limiting variant of the condition. A baby may be born with fractures that occurred in the womb. Growth is often restricted and affected by the condition.	Children – Often of small stature with small arms and legs. Curvature of the spine and frequent fractures are a feature from childhood onwards. Typically need specially adapted wheelchairs and additional support but can still do / achieve things other children can do. Adults – Fewer fractures than in childhood and adolescence, may have respiratory problems due to malformed rib cage and dislocating joints if they also have ligament problems. Often find bending difficult and experience pain due to bone problems.

textbook
training

Type of OI condition	Main features
Type IV This variant falls somewhere between the Type I and Type III condition. Fractures occur but frequency varies between people. Type III is often not diagnosed until a person is older and a clearer picture of their symptoms emerges.	Children may have ligament problems that cause their joints to dislocate. Spinal curvature may occur and is likely to cause a lot of pain. Adults can experience ligament and spinal problems and pain for no obvious reason. They may experience hearing difficulties and have difficulty bending their long bones.

Brittle bone disease (OI) is diagnosed following a physical examination, X-rays and Dexa (bone density) scans and following a detailed medical and family history. Genetic tests can also be used to identify OI in the womb. People living with a type of OI condition are likely to need support and care for their fractures, special care for their brittle teeth, medication and physiotherapy to help reduce pain and may require adapted wheelchairs and other equipment to help with mobility and everyday living activities. Living a healthy lifestyle that includes exercise, weight control, a balanced diet and avoiding smoking and excess alcohol intake can help to prevent some problems and aids recovery from fractures.

People with OI conditions are often able to lead successful and productive lives, achieving all of their goals and ambitions in relation to work, education and their personal life. Support, treatment and adaptations to living and working circumstances are an important part of this but there is no reason to otherwise restrict or have low expectations of a person's opportunities or potential achievements because they have a type of brittle bone disease.

See also – Biological factors; Genetic factors

Bullying

There is no legal definition of bullying in the UK. The UK government defines bullying as behaviour that is:

- repeated
- intended to hurt someone either physically or emotionally
- often aimed at certain groups, eg because of race, religion, gender or sexual orientation (**www.gov.uk**)

Bullies are people who aim to abuse, intimidate or aggressively dominate others. Bullies may use a variety of behaviours in order to gain power over the person or people they are bullying. These may include:

- repeated mocking, taunting or teasing
- physical intimidation or assault
- offensive, degrading, threatening or humiliating comments
- less favourable treatment (discrimination) at work or in social situations
- manipulating, isolating/ignoring or excluding a person

Bullying behaviour is generally disapproved of in UK society and far more people admit to having been bullied than to being bullies or using bullying behaviour themselves. There are four basic types of bullying – emotional; verbal; physical; and cyber-bullying. The use of text messages, email and social networks to bully people has developed alongside the spread of the Internet and the use of mobile phones.

textbook
training

Bullies usually see themselves as having greater social or physical power than the person they bully. Their behaviour is designed to provoke a submissive response from their victim. Bullying can occur in families, at school, in the workplace and in social situations. Bullying incidents can be one-off one-on-one situations or may involve groups of people who create and maintain a buying culture over time.

Victims of bullying have a higher risk of developing stress-related illnesses, suffer damage to their self-esteem and sense of self-worth, may experience loneliness, depression and anxiety and may even consider or actually commit suicide as a result. Efforts should always be made to prevent and tackle incidents of bullying before the victim suffers serious developmental harm.

See also – Adolescence; Peer pressure; Social factors

Chomsky's model

Noam Chomsky is an American cognitive scientist and linguist. Chomsky is best known for his 'universal grammar' theory. This is based on the claim that humans have an inborn brain mechanism that helps them to 'learn' language.

Evidence to support Chomsky's model of language development includes the fact that all children, regardless of the language they're learning, progress through the same step-by-step stages: babbling, saying their first word around the age of one, using two-word combinations from around two-and-a-half to three, and generally accomplishing grammatical rules by four or five.

Chomsky believes that 'learning' a language is essentially a natural rather than a taught process. He believes that the baby's brain contains a genetic package that's triggered by 'environmental' exposure to speech sounds. Once the trigger has been pulled, children go on to eventually start talking by themselves. Provided they are exposed to the right environmental triggers, language acquisition and other skills develop along genetically 'pre-programmed' lines.

Chomsky's claim that the human brain contains a 'language acquisition device' (LAD) is controversial and has been criticised by other linguistic and developmental psychologists. These critics tend to see human language acquisition and development as more strongly influenced by, and perhaps even dependent on, environmental factors and nurturing.

textbook
training

In this sense, language learning depends on being stimulated, taught and corrected by parents, carers, other children and teachers, for example. Skuse (1984) carried out research into children who experienced extreme deprivation and adversity during their early years. Skuse concluded that the development of language is highly vulnerable to deprivation, suggesting there is a critical period for this and that lack of environmental stimuli leads to severely deprived children never acquiring language abilities.

LANGUAGE ACQUISITION

We are designed to walk… That we are taught to walk is impossible. And pretty much the same is true of language. Nobody is taught language. In fact you can't prevent the child from learning it.

Noam Chomsky, The Human Language Serie 2 (1994)

See also – Cognitive development; Biological factors; Environmental factors; Intellectual development; Nature Nurture debate

Reference
Skuse, D (1984), Extreme Deprivation in early childhood – 1. Diverse outcomes for three siblings from an extraordinary family', *Journal of Child Psychology and Psychiatry*, 25(4), 525-41

---

textbook
training

Cognitive development

Cognitive development focuses on the human ability to think and understand, the mental processes that lie behind this ability and the part the brain plays in these processes.

The term *cognition* comes from the Greek word for 'knowing'. Cognitive psychologists believe that behaviour is based on knowing about the situation in which the behaviour occurs. As a result, cognitive theories of development encourage parents and teachers to help children think about what they're doing, thereby appealing to curiosity and interest. Figure 11 summarises the main elements of the cognitive development process.

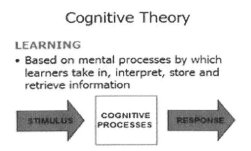

Figure 4 – Cognitive development is concerned with thinking and understanding skills

Cognitive theories of development arose in part to explain how learning involved more than just behavioural reinforcement. Research into how monkeys learn, suggested that motivation to learn isn't only induced by the anticipation of a reward but also by enjoying the learning process itself.

textbook
training

In one study, reported by David Wood (1998), a monkey was being conditioned to pull a lever that sometimes delivered a reinforcer in the form of a peanut. However, when the peanut arrived, the monkey often stored it in its food pouch inside the mouth. As the experiment proceeded, the monkey's food pouch bulged to capacity. But, despite being unlikely to gain from further 'reinforcement', the monkey continued operating the lever. It seemed that the monkey wasn't carrying on with the lever operations to win a reward, but because it found the task interesting!

Cognitive development affects a range of mental, or brain-driven, skills and abilities. These include:

- language acquisition and use
- thinking and problem-solving skills
- attention and focusing
- perception
- memory (storage and recall)
- human intelligence

A focus on cognitive development and the basic idea that information-processing and cognition are fundamentally *human* experiences are central to the cognitive perspective within psychology. Problems and difficulties with cognitive development are an important feature of learning disability and specific learning difficulties

See also – Intellectual development; Piaget's theory; Conservation

Reference
Wood, D (1998), *How Children think and learn*, Oxford, Blackwell

textbook
training

Conservation

Conservation is a concept used by Jean Piaget to describe the capacity for logical thinking. In particular, conservation involves the ability to work out that a certain quantity (200ml of liquid, for example) will remain the same when it is transferred from one type or shape of container such as a short, wide glass (like in figure A, for example) into another narrower, taller glass (like in Figure B, for example).

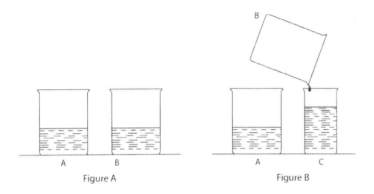

Figure A   Figure B

Figure 5 – An illustration of Piaget's conservation experiment

Piaget argued that children in the pre-operational stage of intellectual development (age 2-7) are not capable of logical thinking so they will assume that the amount of liquid has changed because it looks different in each container. Piaget claimed children who are in the concrete operational stage of intellectual development (age 7 – 11) do understand conservation (that the amount of liquid stays the same) because they have developed logical thinking skills.

See also – Intellectual development; Piaget's theory; Infancy;

textbook
training

Culture

The concept of culture refers to the common values, beliefs and customs or way of life of a group, or sub-group, of people within a particular society or part of society.

The United Kingdom is a diverse, multi-cultural society. It is, for example, ethnically and religiously diverse meaning there are many variants or forms of culture within the UK as a whole. Culture may affect physical growth and development where cultural beliefs or practices influence food choices, patterns of exercise and an individual or group's use of health care services, for example. Social development may also be affected by culture where cultural beliefs or practices influence attitudes, values and opportunities to develop and experience friendships and other non-family relationships.

Grant et al (2005) argue that cultural attitudes to disability have an important impact on the treatment of, and extent to which, disabled people are supported by or stigmatized within a community. Emotional development may also be affected by extended family structures, by the closeness or expected pattern of relationships within the family and by a person's identification with their cultural heritage.

Cultural influences and their developmental impact are often unseen and taken-for-granted by those who experience them. Many people assume that their way of viewing and experiencing the world or relating to others is 'normal' – and it probably is within their own culture. It is only when they cross-cultural comparisons are made that people are able to appreciate that their 'normal' way of living and relating may not be the 'normal' way of being or behaving in a different cultural context. Cross-cultural research have provided good evidence of this.

For example, Beatrice and John Whiting (1975) studied 3-10 year olds in six small communities in Kenya, the Phillipines, America, Mexico, India and Japan. They found that Kenyan, Mexican and Philippine children were the most altruistic and American children the least altruistic. The more individualistic, less community-focused culture of the American children is one explanation given for this finding. There is more need for people to help each other out in poorer countries such as Kenya, Mexico and the Phillipines.

In these different ways, culture can play a very important, though often unseen or taken-for-granted role in shaping our personal growth and development.

See also – Environmental factors; Human development; Social development; Social factors; Nature-Nurture debate

References
Grant, G, Goward, P, Richardson, M and Ramcharan, P (eds) (2005), *Learning Disability: A Life Cycle Approach to Valuing People*, Open University Press,
Whiting, B and Whiting J (1975)., *Children of Six Cultures*, Harvard University Press, Cambridge, MA.

Cystic fibrosis

Cystic fibrosis (CF) is one of the commonest genetic diseases in the UK with roughly 1 in 2500 babies born with the illness. A damaged gene that stops people who carry it from controlling the movement of salt into and out of their body cells properly causes CF. This has effects on the lungs, pancreas and lower gut particularly but can lead to problems all over the body.

In the lungs, the mucus that normally protects the internal surfaces becomes quite thick and sticky. This makes it difficult to move so it clogs up the small tubes and can act as a reservoir for infection. A child with CF often suffers from repeated chest infections that make them weak and slow their growth. Damage to the pancreas can affect appetite and can lead to diabetes mellitus. Again, this can lead to slow growth and a general 'unwellness'. Care staff often refer to this general condition as a 'failure to thrive'.

Recently, new treatments have improved the health of people with CF enormously. A high-calorie diet with added vitamins (A, D, E and K) and a package of enzymes helps with growth. Antibiotics can keep lung infections under control and should be given as soon as the slightest sign of infection occurs. Recent clinical trials have also used genetic engineering techniques to insert undamaged genes into the cells of the lung lining. These genes 'teach' the cells how to control salt movement across the cell membranes. This reduces the thickness of the mucus and so helps to prevent build-up of infection. In the future this may provide a cure for CF.

See also – Genetic factors; Biological factors;

textbook
training

Dementia

Dementia is a general term that is used to describe (or categorise) a range of different medical conditions that affect the structure and functioning of the human brain. This means that there is no condition that is simply called 'dementia'. Instead, 'dementia' is a term used to describe a set of symptoms (a syndrome) caused by a number of different diseases of the brain.

Perhaps the most well-known of these diseases is Alzheimer's disease. Other examples of condition that cause dementia symptoms include vascular dementia, frontotemporal dementia and dementia with Lewy bodies.

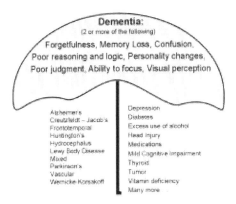

Figure 6 – Dementia is an umbrella term that covers a number of neuro-degenerative brain conditions

Brian Draper, a professor and consultant psychiatrist specialising in old age psychiatry, defines dementia as 'an acquired decline in memory and thinking (cognition) due to brain disease that results in significant impairment of personal, social or occupational function' (2013: 13).

The changes that occur in a person's brain typically lead to:

- death of nerve cells or loss of communication between nerve cells in the brain
- multiple cognitive deficits, including memory impairment
- problems with using language
- failure to recognise people
- problems in orientation – knowing what time of day or year it is and where the person is
- decline in overall mental functioning.

Most dementia-related conditions develop gradually but are progressive and irreversible. This isn't quite the same as saying the symptoms of dementia can't be treated or that the course of a

person's condition or the rate of their decline can't be influenced. Many people are able to 'live well' with dementia for a period of time and can maintain and experience a good quality of life with adaptations to and support within their everyday living environment.

Diagnosing 'dementia'

textbook
training

Initially, and sometimes with hindsight, a person may be aware that their short-term memory (ability to remember recent events) has got worse. This might provoke – or be accompanied by – anxiety and depression, personality and behaviour changes (especially apathy and irritability) and difficulties in personal and/or work relationships as the person becomes less able to cope with the demands of their everyday life.

A person's dementia-based condition is often not diagnosed at this stage. Instead, the person's problems may be viewed as 'stress', anxiety or depression or even 'just part of old age'. When treatment or support for these things fail to resolve the person's problems or their symptoms continue to worsen, further cognitive or neuropsychological tests and brain scans tend to be carried out. These aim to identify whether, and if so how, the person's brain and cognitive functioning have changed. It is usually at this point that a person is diagnosed with a form of 'dementia'.

See also – Ageing process; Cognitive development; Genetic factors; Biological factors
Reference
Draper, B. (2013), *Understanding Alzheimer's Disease and Other Dementias,* Jessica Kingsley Publishers

textbook
training

Diabetes

The term 'diabetes' refers to a group of metabolic disorders in which there are high blood sugar levels over a long period of time. A person who has high blood sugar levels may experience a number of different physical symptoms, including:

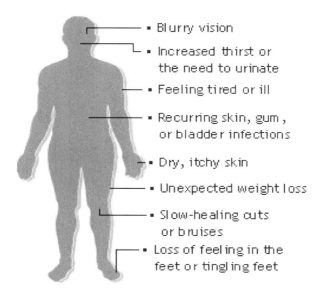

- Blurry vision
- Increased thirst or the need to urinate
- Feeling tired or ill
- Recurring skin, gum, or bladder infections
- Dry, itchy skin
- Unexpected weight loss
- Slow-healing cuts or bruises
- Loss of feeling in the feet or tingling feet

There are two main reasons why a person may develop and experience diabetes. Firstly, a person's pancreas may not produce enough insulin to meet their body's needs (Type 1 diabetes or *diabetes mellitus*). As a result, their blood glucose level may rise above the safe level. To prevent this happening they try to avoid sugary foods and may inject insulin when they know their blood glucose is rising. Insulin is usually injected 2 to 4 times a day and meals and snacks are carefully planned to keep blood sugar within safe limits.

A person with Type I diabetes has to *consciously* do some of the work that the pancreas does automatically in a person without the disease. The cause of Type 1 diabetes is unknown and is generally diagnosed in infancy, childhood or early adolescence. As a result, you may also see or hear it being referred to as 'juvenile diabetes'.

Alternatively, a person's body may not respond appropriately to the insulin that their pancreas is actually producing (Type 2 diabetes or *diabetes insipidus*). As a result, glucose stays in the person's blood, raising their blood glucose levels rather than being moved into the person's cells to produce energy. Type 2 diabetes is also known as 'insulin-resistant' or 'adult-onset diabetes' and is most likely to occur because of excess weight and lack of exercise. Genetic factors also play a part too. A person who has a relative with Type 2 diabetes has a greater risk of developing the condition themselves – the closer the relative (e.g parent or sibling), the greater the risk.

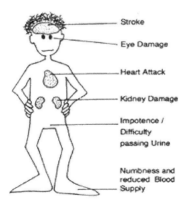

Figure 7 – Possible health effects of chronic diabetes

See also – Genetic factors; Nature Nurture debate; Physical development

---

textbook
training

Discrimination

Unfair discrimination involves treating an individual or group less favourably or unfairly in comparison to another individual or group.

Prejudices relating to gender, 'race' / ethnicity, age, sexuality, disability usually underpin discriminatory behaviour that may be described as sexist (gender-based), racist ('race' / ethnicity-related), ageist (age-biased), homophobic (sexuality-based) or disablist (disability-biased). Discrimination can affect an individual's development in a number of ways. For example, it can:

- damage a person's self-image and self-esteem
- undermine a person's self-confidence and inhibit them from achieving their potential in life
- cause emotional distress and fear
- result in physical assault and injury
- prevent a person from having equal opportunities in education, work or other areas of their social life
- act as a barrier to an individual getting the care services, social support or treatment they need.

See also – Social factors; Self-image; Self-esteem

textbook training

Down's syndrome

Down's syndrome is a genetic disorder caused by a randomly occurring (and not inherited) chromosomal abnormality that affects 1 in 1000 UK babies. Specifically, a person with Down's syndrome has all or part of an additional chromosome 21. As a result, Down's syndrome is also sometimes referred to as Trisomy 21.

Down's syndrome affects physical growth and development as well as intellectual development. A person with Down's syndrome has delayed physical growth and development, characteristic facial features and mild to moderate intellectual disabilities caused by a restricted IQ (intelligence) level. Prenatal screening, including ultrasound, amniocentesis and chorionic villus sampling tests, can identify Down's syndrome during early pregnancy. Some women choose to terminate their pregnancy when they receive a positive result for Down's syndrome, largely because they anticipate the child will be born with significant disabilities. However, this isn't always the case, particularly in countries where there are more positive attitudes to and support services for disabled people.

textbook
training

Supported education and care as well as regular health monitoring are needed by people with Down's syndrome to achieve and maintain a good quality of life. Specialist education, supported work opportunities and sheltered housing are available in the UK for people with Down's syndrome who can benefit from, and want, them. Some people with Down's syndrome do achieve independent living but may also require forms of financial, medical and social support to maintain this. Life expectancy for a person with Down's syndrome in the UK is shorter than average life expectancy at 50-60 years.

A great deal depends on whether a person with Down's syndrome also has a congenital heart defect. Those born without heart problems live longer. In addition to a higher risk of being born with a heart defect, people with Down's syndrome also have higher rates of mental illness, epilepsy and Alzheimer's disease. Visual problems, hearing impairment and chronic ear infections are also common in this group of people.

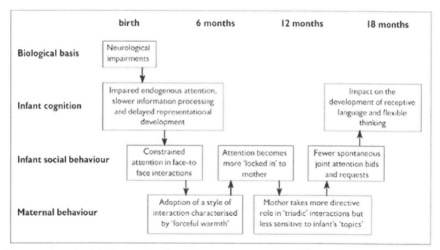

Figure 8 – A child's early development can be affected in various ways by Down's syndrome

Despite the health and development problems that a person with Down's syndrome may experience or be at higher risk of, many people with this condition live satisfying, enjoyable lives and contribute positively to the life of their families and communities through the relationships they form and the voluntary and paid work roles they undertake.

See also – Genetic factors; Nature – Nurture; Infancy; Social development; Intellectual development

Duchenne Muscular Dystrophy

Duchenne muscular dystrophy is a genetically inherited muscular dystrophy condition. A person born with Duchenne muscular dystrophy has inherited gene mutations that lead to progressive muscle weakness and increasing disability.

Duchenne muscular dystrophy is one of the most common forms of muscular dystrophy and typically affects boys in early childhood. Approximately 100 boys are born with Duchenne muscular dystrophy each year in the UK. There are about 2500 boys living with this condition at any one time. Because Duchenne muscular dystrophy is a progressive, life-limiting condition few survive beyond their 20s or early 30s. T

Duchenne muscular dystrophy is present from birth but the symptoms may not be noticed for a few more years. Muscle weakness becomes more evident when a child tries to move independently and struggles to stand up, walk or climb stairs, for example. A GP will need to observe and examine a child, carry out blood tests and refer the child for specialist electrical tests on their muscles in addition to obtaining a muscle biopsy before a diagnosis can be made.

There is no cure for Duchenne muscular dystrophy at present. A number of treatments and forms of support are offered to children and young people living with this condition. These include:

- medication to improve muscle strength and treat heart disorders
- exercise, physiotherapy and mobility aids to assist with basic mobility
- support groups to provide social and emotional support
- surgery to correct postural deformities – particularly scoliosis – that may develop as part of the condition.

The purpose of these treatments and support interventions is to manage an individual's symptoms so they can live as well as possible with the condition they have.

See also – Genetic factors; Nature – Nurture; Infancy; Physical development; Social development; Intellectual development

textbook
training

Economic factors

Economic factors are money-related factors that impact on health and wellbeing.

In addition to income (money earned/ received) and wealth (money and other valuable resources owned), economic factors can include an individual's access to and experiences of employment, the broader impact of the economy on education and work opportunities, living conditions and the funding of public services within society.

Figure 9 – Economic factors have a broad influence on development

Personal development can be affected by economic factors in a number of ways. For example, economic factors (such as level of income) have a strong influence on the kinds of opportunities that a person is able to enjoy in each life stage and are closely linked to health experiences. People who experience poverty, for example, are likely to have poorer physical and mental health experiences and are more likely to die prematurely than people who are classified as being in the higher social classes because of their greater income and wealth.

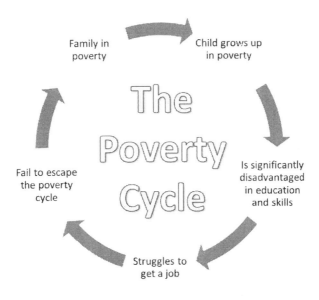

Figure 10 – Children born into poor families can find it very hard to escape from the poverty cycle

See also –Environmental factors; Nature – Nurture debate; Culture; Discrimination; Stress-diathesis model

Egocentrism

Egocentrism is a psychological concept that refers to the way a person perceives the world around them and relates to others. In particular, people who are egocentric see the world only from their own point of view. They do not take into account or appreciate the views, opinions or interests of others. In a simple, narrow way, a person who is egocentric believes they are the centre of attention and that the world, and everyone in it, revolves around them.

Egocentrism is most obvious in the early stages of psychological development when infants and young children often act in a self-centred way, have tantrums and become very upset when their needs, wishes or preferences are not met exactly as they would like by others. Egocentric behaviour is less prominent or frequent in adolescence and adulthood as people learn to appreciate, understand and accept that the needs of others are also important. As people progress through adolescence and early adulthood their ability to control egocentric impulses tends to improve. However, egocentrism can be a lifelong feature or characteristic of the behaviour of people who lack empathy, sensitivity towards others or who are unwilling to deny or delay gratification of their own needs. It can also be a feature of some conditions, such as Huntington's disease, where a person's social skills and ability to read and respond to the emotions of others are affected by underlying brain disease.

See also – Piaget's theory; Self-concept; Self-image; Self-esteem

Emotional development

Emotions are feelings. The process of emotional development refers to the gradual emergence of feelings about self and others. This process begins in infancy with attachment and bonding relationships playing a key part in a child's very early emotional development and also influencing subsequent, lifelong emotional development.

An infant's early emotional development plays an important part in their future relationships with others. Ideally, an infant should have opportunities to develop feelings of trust and security during the early years of life. The process through which these feelings develop is known as attachment.

Emotional development in early childhood

Emotional and social development during childhood builds on the foundations established during infancy. During childhood children try to form new relationships with new people in new situations – such as with teachers at school and with other children who become their friends.

Significant features of social development that occur during childhood include:

- the development of further communication and relationship building skills
- an increase in the number and variety of relationships with people outside of the family
- a greater degree of independence from parents
- an improvement in the ability to use social and language skills to manage personal relationships with others

textbook training

Children gradually develop greater awareness of who they are and how they are similar to and different from others. A child can usually identify their own sex (boy or girl) by the age of two. However, it is not until they reach five or six years of age that most children realise that this feature of their identity is fixed! This concept is known as gender constancy. It forms an important part of a child's developing sense of 'self'.

Emotional development in adolescence

Adolescence is often seen as an emotionally difficult and 'stormy' life stage. Teenagers' turbulent hormones are often blamed for their 'moodiness' and emotional sensitivity.

The significant physical changes that adolescents experience often trigger off concerns about 'being normal' and about self-image. Adolescents tend to need reassurance about their growth patterns. They may seek this from friends, parents, teachers, magazines and other media. The social and emotional consequences of physical maturation during adolescence show how these developmental processes are intertwined rather than separate. For example, early maturation can result in increased attention and extra responsibility, especially for boys. For girls, it can result in unwanted sexual attention, pressure and awkwardness. Alternatively, late maturation can damage self-confidence and self-esteem in some adolescents who feel that they are 'out of sync' with their peers and who may be teased or bullied as a result.

Emotional development in early adulthood

People typically leave home to live independently of their family in early adulthood. Greater independence requires new relationships. Often young adults make new friendships through work and social life, focusing quite strongly on finding a partner and sustaining an intimate relationship. New responsibilities and an extension of the person's social circle may also result from marriage or cohabitation.

Much of adulthood is concerned with trying to find a balance between the competing demands of work, family and friends. Each of these types of relationship contribute to social development by giving the person a sense of connection and belonging to others.

New parenthood is also a feature of early adulthood. For most people it appears to be an experience that brings profound satisfaction, a greater sense of purpose and increased self-worth. It also introduces a number of role changes. Sex roles and spouse relationships tend to change when children arrive. The birth of children appears to result in a drop in partners' relationship satisfaction and an increase in 'role strain' because the roles of partner and spouse are at least partly incompatible.

Emotional development in middle adulthood

Middle adulthood is the life stage when people tend to realize their own mortality. This may be triggered by the death of a parent or the decline in physical abilities. In popular terminology, this life stage is also associated with people having a 'midlife crisis'. There is no research-based evidence for this being a consistent or widely experienced feature of middle adulthood. However, the popular notion is that people in middle adulthood sometimes experience a period of unstable mental health or emotional wellbeing and that dissatisfaction with themselves, their partners or their life situations can lead to dramatic gestures or decisions or changes in their behaviour. Despite this popular misconception, people in middle adulthood generally maintain stable personality characteristics and relationships. They may become more introspective as they re-examine their life and what they have (and still want to) achieved. Changes in family, work and wider social roles also impact on people in this life stage, leading to reconsiderations and adjustments in a person's sense of self and identity.

Emotional development in later adulthood

Partner relationships in later life tend to be based on loyalty, familiarity and mutual investment in the relationship. Partners tend to spend more time with each other. Older women expect to be widowed and to live on their own for a time, older men don't. Older people tend to see their children regularly for purposes of practical help and emotional support. Continuity and adaptation are the themes of later adulthood relationships. Friendships remain important for companionship but there is a reduction in the number of friends as they die.

See also – Attachment;; Parenting style; Self-concept; Self-esteem; Self-image

Environmental factors

In the context of human growth and development, the concept of environmental factors tends to refer to any *external* influence on and individual's growth or development.

In a broad sense, an environmental factor is any influence on human growth or development that exists outside of the human body and which is part of the external world in which a person lives. A person's housing circumstances, their educational opportunities and the parenting style they experience when growing up are all examples of environmental factors that have an influence on their development. By contrast, the genes that a person inherits from their parents, a disease or illness that affects their growth or development or the way their body functions are examples of *internal*, biological influences on development.

Environmental factors have a more indirect and varied impact on human development when compared to genetic and biological influences. However, it is possible to predict in general terms the likely effects that environmental factors such as pollution, poor housing conditions and bullying, for example, can have on human growth and development.

Environmental factors should also be seen as part of the 'nurture' side of the 'nature / nurture debate that is central to the human growth and development is discussed and understood.

See also – Activity theory; Bandura's theory; Economic factors; Lifestyle; Friendships; Nature – Nurture debate; Peer pressure; Social factors

---

textbook
training

Family dysfunction

Family dysfunction is a term used to describe a family in which conflict, behaviour that is destructive or damaging to family members, or the neglect or abuse of children occur regularly is accommodated and becomes accepted by family members as 'normal'. In essence, the family is failing to function in a way that protects and nurtures family members in a socially acceptable way.

The needs of family members living in dysfunctional families may not be met because relationships between family members are inappropriately aggressive, manipulative or unsupportive in other ways. Adults and children living in dysfunctional families may experience high levels of stress, have poor communication skills and feel neglected, emotionally unsupported and have low self-esteem and a distorted or negative sense of self-worth. Adults in dysfunctional families may have substance misuse or mental health problems or have learnt ineffective and inappropriate parenting practices from their own parents. Police and child protection services are likely to intervene in situations where significant family dysfunction is reported to them in order to safeguard the interests of children or vulnerable adults experiencing harm, abuse or neglect.

See also – Emotional development; Social development; Life events; Environmental factors; Self-image; Stress-diathesis model

textbook
training

Fine motor skills

Fine motor skills involve coordinating the movement of small muscles in the wrists, hands, fingers, feet and toes to make precise, detailed movements. Actions such as picking up a pencil, cutting out shapes of paper and tying shoe laces depend on gradually more sophisticated fine motor skills.

Learning to use their hands and fingers is quite a complicated task for babies and young children. It involves skills like:

- Grasping: learning to hold objects securely and precisely (like a rattle, a pencil or a spoon)
- Hand-eye co-ordination: Learning to make their hands work together with what their eyes can see (like fitting a piece into a jigsaw puzzle or building a tower of blocks)
- Manipulation: learning to use their hands and fingers to handle objects precisely (like screwing/unscrewing and threading beads)

Most babies start to play with their hands from about 3 months old. They will spend time just gazing at their hands or may hold a rattle for a short time. Bright, stimulating toys, hung where a baby can see them, (such as a mobile or baby gym) will encourage the baby to reach out and grasp and help to develop hand-eye co-ordination.

By the age of 6 months, most babies will reach out and grasp an object or toy. They will do this using their whole hand, (palmar grasp) and will start to pass toys from one hand to the other. As their fine motor skills develop, babies learn to use their fingers

textbook
training

more precisely. By the age of 9 months, most babies can use their thumb and index finger to pick up small objects using a pincer grasp.

By the age of one year, most babies can point with their index finger and clap their hands together. Fine motor skills will continue to develop through simple play activities and routine self-help skills like feeding and dressing themselves. By the age of 18 months, most babies can scribble with a crayon and feed themselves with a spoon, (which requires a great deal of hand-eye co-ordination and may be very messy to begin with!).

Most 2 year olds can build a tower of 5 or 6 blocks and turn the pages in a book one at a time, (a difficult manipulative task). By the age of 3 years, most children will be starting to use a dominant hand (either right or left-handed) and can hold a crayon using a tripod grasp. They can also thread large beads onto a string and feed themselves using a fork and spoon.

As muscle strength increases in the hands and fingers, children can use their fine motor skills for more complex tasks. By the age of 4 years, most children can use a pencil to draw a figure with a head, legs and a body, complete a large piece jigsaw puzzle and can cut with safety scissors. At 5 years old, these skills have improved even further and most children can feed themselves with a knife and fork, fasten and unfasten buttons and colour in pictures, staying within the lines.

See also – Infancy; Human growth; Milestones; Biological factors; Nature – Nurture debate; Klinefelter syndrome; Play

textbook
training

Friendships

A friendship is a platonic relationship between two people who know, like and trust each other. Generally, friendships develop between people who are unrelated to each other and who share common interests or values. Friendships tend to be based on each person liking and being supportive of each other.

In the context of human development, relationships with friends become increasingly important during childhood. In fact, by the middle of childhood many children prefer to spend time with their peers rather than their parents and can become quite embarrassed by parental attention when their friends are around! Childhood friendships tend to be very sex-segregated with boys preferring to make friends with other boys and girls establishing friendships with other girls.

Relationships with friends go on to play a very important role in social and emotional development during adolescence. Friendships are more stable and adolescents generally spend more time with their peers than they did during childhood. An adolescent's attitudes and values, ways of behaving and sense of self-worth is significantly affected by their friendships and peer group expectations. An adolescent's friendship group becomes a means of transition from family to independent, adult life. It is through using their increasing social opportunities and their ability to choose and make new relationship with peers that adolescents gradually separate from their parents.

Often young adults make new friendships through work and social life, focusing quite strongly on finding a partner and sustaining an intimate relationship.

Friendships are very important in children's and adolescent's social and emotional development and play a vital role in supporting and sustaining an adult's sense of identity, belonging and sense of self-esteem.

See also –Social development; Emotional development; Peer pressure; Adolescence

textbook training

Genetic factors

Genetics is a branch of biology that deals with heredity, particularly the transmission of genes and genetic variation (similarities and differences) between organisms (like human beings!). The term genetic factors tends to be used to refer to the influence that genes – the molecular units of heredity – have on an individual's pattern or experience of growth and development.

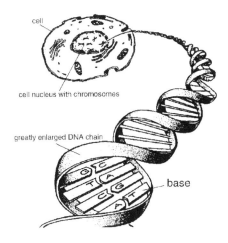

Figure 11 – DNA chains carry and transmit human genetic information.

Nature influences on human growth and development include genetic factors and biological processes that affect the person from within. People who take a more extreme 'nature' viewpoint, argue that we are pre-programmed by our genes and biological processes to develop and behave in certain ways. By contrast,

When you next see a baby, you will be looking at the unique product of two different, but now combined, sets of genes. In purely biological terms, a baby consists of cells. With the exception of egg and sperm cells, each cell of the human body contains 46 chromosomes that are arranged in 23 pairs. In turn, chromosomes contain genes. Genes are units of heredity information. That is, they pass on information that affects biological characteristics like our eye colour and our predisposition to particular conditions (see table 00). We know this from scientific research that has identified and isolated the specific genes responsible for eye-colour and for these particular conditions.

Because you have 23 pairs of chromosomes, you also have matching pairs of genes for nearly every biological trait. Twenty-two of the pairs, known as autosomes, look alike and can be matched. For these twenty-two genes, the instructions of the dominant gene are followed rather than those of the so-called recessive gene. A recessive gene's instructions are only followed if neither in its pair is dominant.

The features and characteristics that a person inherits are generally those that are genetically dominant. The twenty third pair of chromosomes that are not autosomes, are the sex chromosomes. They are different to the autosomes because they can be one of two types: X or Y chromosomes. A woman's egg cells only carry X chromosomes. The sperm cells from the father can carry an X or a Y chromosome. It is therefore the father's sperm cells that determine whether a child will be male or female. If the sperm cell that fertilises the egg cell carries an X chromosome, the XX combination will make the child female. If the sperm cell carries a Y chromosome, the child will have an XY combination and will be male.

Gender determination		mother	
		X	X
father	X	XX	XX
	Y	XY	XY

Figure 12 – An illustration of how a child's gender is genetically determined

It is fair to say that genes do exert a powerful influence on the physical growth and development of human beings. However, lots of other factors also interact with our genetic predispositions to influence the way we develop. For example, while an individual might inherit a genetic predisposition to a particular form of cancer or to heart disease, the person's lifestyle can make it more or less likely that disease will actually occur. So, while genes play an important part in determining who we are and how we grow and develop, the environment in which we live is also very influential.

Advances in genetic research are continually revealing how genes combine and work together to make some people susceptible to certain diseases. In addition to genes, lots of other factors also interact with our genetic predispositions to influence the way we develop. For example, while an individual might inherit a genetic predisposition to a particular form of cancer or to heart disease, the person's lifestyle can make it more or less likely that disease will

textbook
training

actually occur. So, while genes play an important part in determining who we are and how we grow and develop, the environment in which we live is also very influential.

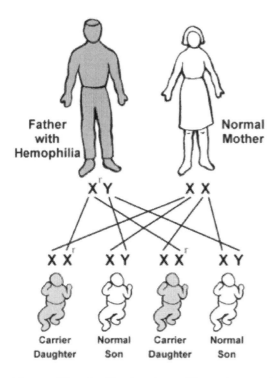

Examples of conditions that some people are genetically predisposed to include haemophilia (see diagram), cystic fibrosis and coeliac disease.

Advances in genetic research are continually revealing how genes combine and work together to make some people susceptible to certain diseases.

Figure 13 – An illustration of how hemophilia is inherited

See also – Cystic fibrosis; Brittle bone disease; Down's syndrome; Duchenne Muscular dystrophy; Phenylketonuria (PKU); Diabetes; Huntington's disease, Klinefelter's syndrome; Nature / Nurture debate

Gessell's theory

Arnold Gessell (1880 – 1961) outlined a theory of human development based on the claim that development occurred as a result of maturational processes. In effect, human development occurs in response to a sequence of biologically-based changes in the human body – especially the brain. The individual is seen as maturing through several different but linked stages of growth and development in which a predictable, biologically-based 'programme' of maturation unfolds. For example, foetal development during pregnancy follows a fixed, predictable set of stages until the foetus is ready to be born. From birth, a genetic 'programme' leads to the baby developing into a child and the child into an adolescent. Maturational processes then lead on to developmental changes occurring in adulthood and finally a progression into old age.

Gessell claimed that this process of change and development follows a relatively predictable pattern because it is 'hard wired' into the human genome. From this perspective, maturational processes drive human physical, psychological and emotional development with the environment providing only background support rather than playing a leading role. This contrasts with humanistic and learning theory where nurture effects are seen as having a more important influence on the individual's development.

See also – Nature / Nurture; Maturation; Biological factors

textbook
training

Gross Motor Skills

Gross motor skills refer to movement and coordination of the head, large limbs (the arms and legs) and the body. These skills are required for crawling, walking and running.

An infant's physical growth and development follows a predictable pattern. Physical change occurs from the head downwards (cephalocaudal) and from the middle of the body outwards (proximodistal). As a result, an infant will first develop gross motor skills – basic, unsophisticated movement of their limbs, trunk and head – that enable them to hold their head up without support, to hold on to people and large objects and later to crawl about. Gross motor skills always occur before, and provide a basic foundation for, fine motor skills.

By the age of 3 months, most babies have developed head control and can lift their head up if they are lying on their stomach (prone position). They will start to use their leg muscles by kicking, especially when lying on their back or when supported in the bath.
The muscles of the upper body are the next to develop and this involves the baby gaining control of their arms, hands and back muscles. By the age of 6 months, most babies can sit up with some support and can roll over. They will also start to use their arms to reach out for toys and other objects and are beginning to bear weight on their legs when held securely by an adult.

Not all babies crawl, but most babies find their own way of moving around, such as rolling over and over or shuffling on their bottom. By the age of 9 months, most babies will have developed some way

textbook
training

of getting around! The development of standing and walking requires muscle strength, balance and co-ordination. Babies need lots of opportunities to practice these skills as their confidence develops and they are finally ready to walk by themselves. By the age of 18 months, most babies will walk sturdily alone, but some will still need to hold on to an adult's hand for extra support.

As the child's movements become more co-ordinated, they will start to be more adventurous and will experiment with climbing and getting up and down stairs, (although some will have attempted this much earlier). By the age of 2 years, most children will be able to climb confidently onto furniture and walk up and down stairs, using both feet on each step. Playing outside will give toddlers lots of opportunities to practice these new skills and they will enjoy sit and ride toys, running around and learning how to kick a ball.

Children gain more control over their movements as their gross motor skills continue to develop. By the age of 3 years, most children can pedal a tricycle and jump with both feet together. Their body co-ordination will be improving rapidly and they will enjoy trying to catch a large ball, walking on tiptoe and running around obstacles.

Children need lots of stimulation and opportunities to practice their gross motor skills in a safe environment. Lots of praise and encouragement will also help children to gain confidence and enjoy developing their physical abilities. They need space to move around and adult support to help them improve their skills.

By the age of 4 years, most children can walk up and down stairs like an adult, pedal and control a tricycle with confidence and throw, catch and kick a ball with some accuracy. These abilities become more advanced and skillful as the child reaches 5 years old, when most children can skip, hop and play bat and ball games with good co-ordination.

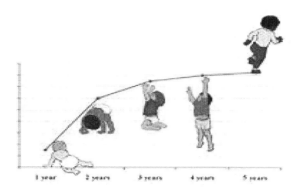

Figure 14 Examples of motor skills developed during infancy and childhood

See also – Infancy; Human growth; Human development; Milestones; Biological factors; Nature – Nurture debate; Klinefelter syndrome; Play

textbook
training

High blood pressure

Blood pressure is the force that the blood in the circulatory system exerts against the walls of the arteries. High blood pressure is a persistently elevated blood pressure. The medical term for high blood pressure is 'hypertension'.

Blood pressure is measured in millimetres of mercury (mmHg) using an electronic or manual blood pressure monitor. The monitor takes two measurements and the person's blood pressure is then recorded as two figures, such as 140/80. The force, or pressure, which the blood puts on the walls of the artery when the heart beats and pushes the blood out into the circulatory system is the first of these measurements. This is known as the *systolic* blood pressure and is the larger or first number in the blood pressure reading. The continuous pressure that the person's blood puts on the arteries between heart beats is the second measurement and smaller number. Technically, this is known as the *diastolic* blood pressure.

A healthy young adult will have a blood pressure reading of 120/80 mmHg (millimetres of mercury) or below but anything under 130/80 mmHg is considered normal. A person is considered to have high blood pressure (hypertension) when their blood pressure is consistently recorded as 180/110 mmHg or higher. In most cases people who have high blood pressure are unaware that they are hypertensive as there are no obvious, definitive symptoms. Some people with high blood pressure do get regular headaches, experience shortness of breath and get blurred vision because of it. However, most people only find out they are hypertensive when their blood pressure is measured by a healthcare or fitness professional. People who have high blood pressure are at increased risk of having a stroke, developing heart disease or kidney failure.

Where there is no specific, easily identifiable cause of a person's high blood pressure, a medical practitioner is likely to diagnose primary or essential hypertension. A number of factors increase a person's risk of developing primary hypertension including:

- Age – risk increases with age
- A family history of high blood pressure
- Being of African or Caribbean origin
- High salt intake
- Being overweight or obese
- Smoking
- Large alcohol intake

High blood pressure that is caused by another underlying medical or physical health problem is known as secondary hypertension. For example, people who have kidney disease, diabetes or Cushing's syndrome or who use recreational drugs such as cocaine or amphetamines may experience high blood pressure as a result of this.

Eating a balanced diet low in salt and fat but high in fibre, fruit and vegetables, staying within recommended intake levels for alcohol, reducing tea and coffee intake, avoiding smoking, maintaining a healthy weight and taking regular exercise are all effective ways to prevent or reduce high blood pressure. People who are unable to reduce their high blood pressure by making lifestyle changes may be prescribed one or more types of blood pressure-lowering medication by their GP.

See also – Biological factors; Stress-diathesis model; Genetic factors

Holmes-Rahe rating scale

The Holmes-Rahe stress rating scale, also known as the *Social Readjustment Rating Scale* (SRRS), is a list of life events that have been identified as triggers to the development of illness.

Psychiatrists Thomes Holmes and Richard Rahe (1967) constructed the SRRS using data from obtained from the medical records of 5000 people. People were asked to rate 43 life events in order of stressfulness. Holmes and Rahe examined the ratings alongside the medical records of the people involved and found that there was a significant link between people's perceptions and experiences of stressful life events and subsequent illness. The SRRS has been tested several times by other researchers who have obtained similar results. This indicates that it is a reliable data collection tool and that the data obtained are valid.

The Holmes and Rahe SRRS measures stress by allocating a number of "Life Change Units" to specific life events that have occurred in the past 12 months. A person's score gives a rough estimate of how likely they are to become ill because of stress. The scoring system for is as follows:

- Score of 300+: At risk of illness.
- Score of 150-299: Risk of illness is moderate. (reduced by 30% from the above risk)
- Score <150: Slight risk of illness.

See also – Life events; Stress-diathesis model
Reference
Holmes TH, Rahe RH (1967). *"The Social Readjustment Rating Scale". Journal of Psychosomatic Research* **11** *(2): 213–8*

textbook
training

Hormones

Hormones are chemical substances secreted into the blood by the endocrine glands (see table 00 below). These substances stimulate activity in other organs. For example, males and females both secrete the hormones oestrogen and testosterone as a natural part of their physical functioning. Males secrete more testosterone than females whilst females secrete more oestrogen than males.

Hormones are a particularly important influence on growth and development during adolescence. As a result of increased hormone production, physical growth and development occur in the primary and secondary sexual characteristics of both boys and girls during adolescence. The differences in levels of hormonal secretions largely account for differences in physical growth and development in this phase.

Figure 15 – Hormones impact on both primary and secondary sexual characteristics

Sex	Primary	Secondary
Male	Penis	Voice lowers
	Scrotum	Public hair develops
Female	Ovaries	Breasts develop
	Uterus	Hips widen
	Vagina	Pubic hair grows
	Clitoris	
	Labia	

At the end of puberty, hormonal activity slows down and the rate of physical change reduces dramatically as a result.

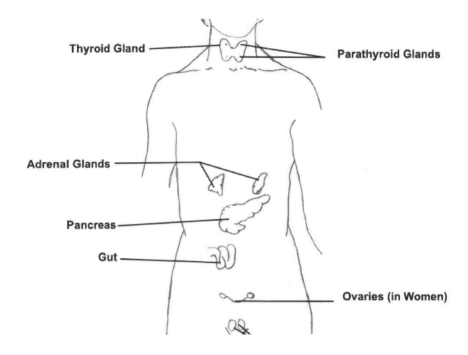

Figure 16 – Location of key endocrine glands

See also – Biological factors; Human development; Puberty; Nature – Nurture debate; Maturity; Oestrogen

textbook training

Human Development

Human development refers to changes in the complexity, sophistication and use of a person's capabilities and skills.

Human development includes changes that go beyond improvements in a person's physical capabilities and skills. From the moment of birth, human beings experience a continuous process of physical, intellectual, social and emotional development so that development is never complete. It is the complex interaction of physical processes and capabilities with social, emotional and intellectual stimuli and experiences that triggers and shapes human development. Some of this complexity is captured by the nature-nurture debate that focuses on whether and how nature (biological / genetic) and nurture (environmental / social / cultural) factors impact on the way a person develops.

See also – Biological factors; Environmental factors; Genetic factors; Social factors; Human growth; Intellectual development; Emotional development; Social development; Milestones; Maturity

textbook
training

Human growth

Human beings experience growth when they increase in physical size or 'mass'.

Human growth is a gradual process that occurs from birth up until a point in early adulthood where we reach our maximum height. Robert Wadlow, an American man, is the tallest person ever. His height was recoded at 272cm or 8.92 feet tall. The tallest ever woman, Zeng Jinlian, measured 248cm or 8.17 feet tall when she died in China in 1982. A person who grows to an exceptional height, like Robert Wadlow or Zeng Jinlian, usually has a medical condition resulting from genetic or endocrine system abnormalities. Average adult height is approximately 5 feet 10 inches for men in the UK and five feet 4 inches for women.

As you are no doubt aware, some people don't stop getting bigger just because they've stopped getting taller! The physical process of human growth involves both height and weight gain. However, once we reach our maximum height, other aspects of our physique are also usually fully evolved and have reached a point of physical maturity. Eating and drinking too much and being inactive can result in further weight increases once our body has reached this point of physical maturity. Increases in size for these reasons are not part of the normal or expected pattern of human growth.

See also – Biological factors; Genetic factors; Environmental factors; Nature-Nurture debate; Hormones; Puberty; Milestones

Huntington's disease

Huntington's disease is a neurodegenerative disorder that is caused by a genetically transmitted gene mutation. The condition gradually impairs a person's muscle coordination, mental abilities and behavioural control.

The onset of Huntington's disease symptoms is subtle and often not noticed except by the person themselves and those very close to them. Early symptoms include mild mood or cognitive (memory, thinking, decision-making) problems. A more obvious unsteady gait and poor physical coordination follow. The characteristic symptoms of uncoordinated, jerky movements of the neck, arms and legs, physical rigidity and declining mental abilities gradually appear over a twenty-year period after the initial onset of symptoms. Behavioural control problems related to apathy, irritability, anxiety and depressed mood are also often a feature of a person's declining ability to function independently. Both the physical and mental symptoms described result from the gradual failure of the person's brain to function normally. In particular, neurological changes prevent the brain from creating, sending and controlling 'signals' to other parts of the person's body. This is why a person's movement and mental state become difficult for them to control.

Frequent falls, increased risk of heart disease and pneumonia and the onset of dementia reduces the life expectancy of a person with Huntington's disease to approximately twenty years following the initial onset of their symptoms. People are typically aged between thirty-five and forty-four years of age when they first experience symptoms but may be younger or older than this in some cases.

textbook
training

As there is currently no cure and little effective medication, people with Huntington's disease require increasing levels of support and care to function. Many people are able to live independently for a long time if they receive assistance from family and friends or are able to obtain appropriate services. However, the very high levels of basic care and assistance required usually leads to people being supported in full-time residential care during the latter stages of their life.

See also – Genetic factors; Biological factors

Infancy

Infancy is the first life stage following birth. It is generally thought to cover the first two years of life and is a very active stage of growth and development. Major changes occur in the physical, intellectual, emotional and social areas of a child's development during infancy.

Physical growth and development during infancy

Physical growth and development is rapid during the first phase of the life span. Between birth and eighteen months of age a child will grow to be XX its birth weight. Rapid growth occurs in all the major body systems so that by the age of eighteen months the child is very different in terms of appearance and physical capabilities to when he/she was born.

Some of the key physical changes that affect both the physical appearance and capability of a child in the first eighteen months of life are those that occur in bone and muscles. A new-born baby has very soft bones with a high water content. Ossification, or hardening, of the bones is a gradual process that occurs sufficiently quickly in the first eighteen months of life to change a baby from a floppy, helpless state to one where it can move and sit up independently. Two terms are used to describe the overall pattern in which human physical growth occurs. These are cephalocaudal (from the head downwards) and proximodistal (from the trunk outwards).

The first eighteen months of life involve a spurt in the developing complexity of organs, such as the brain, and the nervous system as well as the changes in body size and shape that can clearly be seen.

By the time that the child has reached 18 months of age the physical changes that have happened will provide a basis on which motor (movement) skills can develop.

Motor development refers to the movement skills and abilities that human beings develop. Early motor development includes the emergence of:

- locomotor patterns   pulling, crawling, walking (holding on)
- non-locomotor patterns holding head up, pushing, bending body
- manipulative skills   reaching, grasping, stacking blocks

The movement skills that first develop during infancy are the gross motor skills. These are the basic, unsophisticated but important abilities that allow the child to control movement of their limbs, trunk and head. They give the infant the ability to reach out, hold their head up independently and roll over without help for example. These skills are gradually added to during infancy, adolescence and adulthood as the individual develops fine motor skills. These are the sophisticated, highly skilled and controlled minor movements that many everyday activities (eating with cutlery, and getting dressed, for example) depend on.

The expected pattern of physical growth during infancy is sometimes referred to as 'normal development'. Whilst children grow, that is put on weight and get taller, at different rates during infancy, large-scale, long term studies of patterns of growth have provided care practitioners with data on average and normal rates of growth. This data has been used to produce centile charts of height and weight for both male and female infants.

Emotional development during infancy

An infant's early emotional development plays an important part in their future relationships with others. Ideally, an infant should have opportunities to develop feelings of trust and security during the early years of life. The process through which these feelings develop is known as attachment. This involves an infant developing a strong emotional link with her parents or main caregivers. The parent or carer response to this emotional linking is known as bonding. It is through attachment and bonding that an infant's first emotional relationship is formed.

An infant's response to others changes as they develop socially and emotionally:

- up to 6 months, anyone can hold the baby. The baby may protest when put down by whoever is holding them. This is known as indiscriminate attachment.
- between 7 and 12 months the baby is usually bonded to her parents and shows fear of strangers. This can be intense for 3 or 4 months. This is known as specific attachment.
- from 12 months onwards the baby's attachments broaden to include other close relatives and people whom they see frequently. This is known as multiple attachment.

It is thought that our first experience of attachment and bonding provides a 'blueprint' for subsequent relationships. Poor or faulty attachment, or problems with parental bonding, may lead to feelings of insecurity and difficulties in forming and maintaining relationships later in life. As their social and intellectual abilities develop, infants are increasingly able to communicate and interact with other people.

textbook
training

This is partly the result of the increasing experience that infant's gain of other people and the world around them. However, making friends and playing co-operatively also require some practice. Opportunities to mix and play with other children have a positive effect on the development of an infant's relationship-building skills.

Intellectual development during infancy

Thinking is an intellectual, or cognitive, activity. During early infancy babies tend to respond mainly to physical stimuli. They cry when they are wet, cold and hungry, for example. This is a relatively primitive level of intellectual response. Jean Piaget, a Swiss Psychologist who studied and wrote about cognitive development, called infancy the sensorimotor stage of intellectual development. He claimed that infants learn about the world by using their senses (touch, hearing, sight, smell and taste – hence 'sensori') and through physical activity (hence 'motor'). There is very limited cognitive or intellectual activity involved in this type of learning. For example, infants don't deliberately plan or use their memories and experiences in a conscious way.

Thinking skills gradually improve as an infant grows older and experiences intellectual development. For example, by the end of infancy, a child will learn that people and objects continue to exist in the world even when they can't be seen. This is known as object permanence. In contrast, a baby who is less than eight months old won't usually search for a toy that they see 'hidden' from view in front of them.

This is because they haven't usually developed the thinking ability to know that the toy still exists. In fact, it no longer seems to exist at all! An older infant or young child will look for a toy hidden in this way because their intellectual development enables them to work out that objects don't usually just stop existing in the world because they're out of sight.

Figure 17 – Intellectual development during infancy

Age	Developmental change
Birth	A baby explores, using their senses to learn.
1 month	A baby is able to recognise their parents or main carers by sight and smell.
3 months	A baby learns by playing with their hands, holding and grasping objects.
6 months	An infant is aware of their parent or carers voice and can take part in simple play activities.
9 months	An infant recognises familiar toys and pictures, joins in games with familiar people and is able to respond to simple instructions.
12 months	An infant can copy other people's behaviour and is able to use objects (e.g brush or spoon) appropriately.
15 months	An infant can remember people, recognise and sort shapes and knows some parts of body ('Where is your nose?').
18 months	An infant is able to recognise themselves in a picture or reflection, can respond to simple instructions and is able to remember and recall simple information.
2 years	A child can complete simple jigsaws and develops a basic understanding of the consequences of their actions.
2 ½ years	A child is now usually very inquisitive, asking lots of questions, knows their own name and can find details in pictures.
3 years	A child can usually understand time, is able to recognise different colours, can compare the size of different objects (bigger, smaller) and is able to remember the words to their favourite songs and rhymes.

textbook
training

Developing language skills

Learning the basics of a spoken language is an important part of intellectual development during infancy. Babies begin developing communication skills almost straight from birth. Smiles, movements and noises quickly become ways of communicating with care-givers. Babies can also receive information and communicate their feelings from a very early age. Words don't usually become a feature of communication before an infant is one-year old. First words are proceeded by lots of 'babbling'. Once an older infant begins using words they will quickly develop their vocabulary, putting words into short sentences, and learning a few new words each day.

Social development during infancy

As their social and intellectual abilities develop, infants are increasingly able to communicate and interact with other people. This is partly the result of the increasing experience that an infant gains of other people and the world around them. However, making friends and playing co-operatively also require some practice. Opportunities to mix and play with other children have a positive effect on the development of an infant's relationship-building skills.

See also – Attachment; Piaget's theory; Chomsky's model; Bandura's theory; Conservation; Emotional development; Play; Sibling rivalry

textbook
training

Intellectual development

Intellectual development is defined as the process of developing thinking, language and other cognitive abilities, such as memory.

Human intellectual development affects both the quantity and the quality of what an individual can do with their brain. People used to believe that a child was born with a mind like an empty book. It was thought that the 'book' gradually filled up with knowledge as the child experienced the world around it. However, scientific research has shown that babies start learning in the womb and already have some basic abilities and lots of potential at the moment of their birth. Jean Piaget (1896 – 1980), a Swiss psychologist, first put forward the theory that we are born with basic intellectual abilities that improve as we experience different stages of intellectual development during infancy, childhood and adolescence.

Jean Piaget, the Swiss Psychologist, argued that human beings first develop the ability to use 'symbols' in the form of images and words during early childhood. As a child's intellectual abilities develop, they become better at using and manipulating these 'symbols'. This pattern of progressive intellectual development can be seen in the way that children's play becomes more imaginative and sophisticated throughout childhood. A broom can become 'a horse' or a doll can be used to represent 'mummy'.

See also – Cognitive development; Piaget's model; Conservation; Infancy; Adolescence

textbook training

Klinefelter syndrome

This is a genetic condition, also known as XXY syndrome, that only affects boys.

Klinefelter syndrome arises from having an additional X chromosome. This is not inherited but happens randomly during formation of the egg, sperm or developing foetus. The additional X chromosome interferes with the development of the testicles. As a result, adult males have a reduced ability to produce testosterone and may experience developmental and fertility problems.

Symptoms of low energy, excess abdominal fat, lack of muscle and a low sex drive are often not noticed until puberty. However, other features of this condition may be noticed earlier including being born with undescended testicles, being slow to sit up unaided and slow to crawl, being quiet and relatively passive and using language later than expected. Learning difficulties (with reading, writing, spelling) and problems forming friendships and expressing feelings may be a feature of adolescence. Adult males may only be diagnosed with Klinefelter syndrome when seeking help for fertility problems.

There is no cure as the additional X chromosome can't be removed from a carrier's cells. Treatments and interventions aim to overcome some of the deficits and problems that the condition causes. Examples of these include:

- Testosterone replacement medication
- Educational psychology interventions for learning difficulties
- Physiotherapy to develop physique and motor skills
- Exercise to develop physique and fitness

- Counselling to provide emotional support with fertility issues
- Speech and language therapy to overcome developmental delay and promote use of speech.

Klinefelter syndrome does not have an impact on intellectual development or the length of a person's lifespan.

See also – Genetic factors; Biological factors; Puberty; Adolescence

textbook
training

Life events

A life event is a significant event that changes a person's status, circumstances, perceptions or experience of themselves to the extent that it influences or shapes their personal development.

A life event can be a pivotal moment that affects the direction of a person's life or personal development. This could occur in any life stage and may well mark a change in life stage. Predictable life events, such as starting school, going through puberty and retiring from work, often mark a transition from one stage of life to another and act as milestones in our personal development, for example. Unpredictable life events, such as sudden illness or injury, redundancy and the death of a friend or relative, occur unexpectedly, are often associated with loss but may also lead to positive change in a person's life.

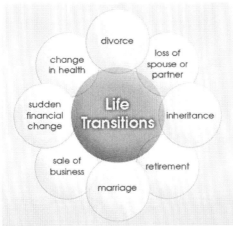

Figure 18 – Examples of events that can result in life transitions.

See also – Holmes and Rahe scale; Stress-diathesis model; Human development; Psychological change

textbook
training

Lifespan

Life span is the length of time between a person's birth and their death.

According to valid and credible records the maximum human life span ever achieved is 122 years. It is very unusual for human beings to survive to such an advanced age. The more typical human lifespan is, in fact, revealed by another concept - life expectancy. This refers to the number of years that a man or woman living in a specified country can expect to live at any given point in time. The life expectancy at birth for men born in the United Kingdom in 2006 was 77. It is slightly longer, at 82 years, for women born in the United Kingdom in 2006.

Life expectancy at birth has increased significantly for both men and women over the last few centuries (see figure 00) and is continuing to do so slowly. Despite this, the length of the human life span has not been lengthened. It is still not possible to live forever or to hang on to eternal youth! Human beings inevitably age and eventually die. The good news, however, is that more people than ever are living out their life span potential rather than dying prematurely.

See also – Biological factors; Genetic factors; Environmental factors; Ageing process; Maturity; Nature – Nurture debate

textbook
training

Life stage

A life stage is an age-related period of human growth and development.

Each human life stage is thought to encompass a distinctive pattern of human growth and development. The classic human life stages that are referred to in health and social care theory and practice are infancy (0-3 years), childhood (4-9 years), adolescence (10-18 years), adulthood (19-65) and older adulthood (65+).

Dividing human growth and development into stages like these is a common way of identifying the main developmental patterns and points of transition that people tend to experience during the human lifespan. Health and social care services are often organized and provided for 'client groups' that are based on these life stages. The assumption is that those in a particular life stage have similar health and social care needs.

See also – Lifespan; Human development; Human growth; Ageing process; Maturity; Adolescence; Infancy

textbook
training

Lifestyle

Lifestyle refers to the way a person lives. This can include the habits, attitudes, tastes, moral standards and behaviour a person or group of people has.

The lifestyles of 'healthy' people are often seen to be distinctive and different from the lifestyles of 'unhealthy' people. Lifestyle is also associated with the consumption or use of a whole variety of things that affect human health and development. These range from the foods we consume, to the use of alcohol, drugs and cigarettes. In this sense, lifestyle factors refer to both our attitudes and to our behaviour.

Figure 19 -Various lifestyle factors and choices are linked to health and wellbeing.

See also – Environmental factors; Human development; Culture; Social factors

Maturity

Maturity is the point at which a human being achieves their physical (bodily) and/or psychological potential. This is generally achieved in early adulthood though there is no fixed or specific age.

Maturation theory is an example of a nature approach to human growth and development. This claims that a process of physical growth and development unfolds from birth and continues through the various stages of the human life course due to natural, pre-programmed 'maturation' processes. As such, maturation is seen as a predictable sequence of changes in the human body that is controlled by genes.

See also – Gessell, Human development, Human growth; Nature – Nurture debate; Puberty; Ageing process.

Menopause

Menopause is the period in a woman's life when menstruation stops permanently and she is no longer able to have children. This is usually between 45 and 55 years of age. A woman is defined as being menopausal a year after her last period, with no subsequent episodes of menstrual flow occurring.

The onset of the menopause is one of the major physical changes experienced by women during adulthood. The menstrual cycle generally ceases because the woman's ovaries no longer produce the hormones that are necessary for ovulation and menstruation. Menopause may occur earlier in women who smoke cigarettes, who have had chemotherapy treatment or who have had their ovaries or uterus removed for other medical reasons. On average, women experience the menopause around the age of 50, though there is some variation with earlier and later onsets occurring.

See also – Physical development; Perimenopause; Hormones; Oestrogen

Milestones

A milestone is a notable, significant stage or event in a person's development.

In many respects the process of human growth and development follows a fairly predictable pattern. For example, observation, experience and research tell us that specific growth and development changes tend to occur within particular time periods (see figure 00). We also know that human growth and development follow a predictable sequence. We know, for example, that when a baby can sit up without support they will next develop the ability to crawl followed by the ability to stand up and finally the ability to walk. Linking this sequence of expected growth and development 'events' to an expected timeframe enables us to talk about developmental norms or 'milestones'.

Milestone	Age
Baby can sit unaided	6-9 months
Baby can crawl	8-10 months
Baby can walk unaided	12-13 months
Infant can say a few words	9-12 months
Puberty begins	10 (girls) 12 (boys)
Menopause occurs	45 – 55 years

Figure 20 Examples of developmental norms or 'milestones'

See also – Infancy; Physical development; Nature-Nurture debate; Motor skills; Human growth; Human development; Klinefelter syndrome

textbook
training

Nature / nurture debate

The nature/nurture debate is a longstanding debate about the relative importance of 'nature' and 'nurture' factors in human growth and development.

The nature/nurture debate provides two important ways of explaining human growth and development:

- the 'nature' approach suggests that people are born with qualities, abilities and characteristics that determine the kind of person they will become. These key influences on development are seen as occurring naturally.
- the 'nurture' approach argues that it is the way a person is brought up, their experience of the world and the circumstances they live in that are a more important influence on the kind of person they become. These key influences are not naturally occurring but are the result of luck, opportunity and human activity.

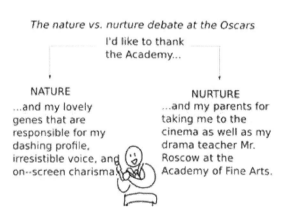

Figure 21 – Nature and nurture influences in action?

Nature influences on human growth and development include genetic factors and biological processes that affect the person from within. People who take a more extreme 'nature' viewpoint, argue that we are pre-programmed by our genes and biological processes to develop and behave in certain ways. By contrast, nurture influences are non-biological, environmental factors that affect the person from outside. People who take a more extreme 'nurture' viewpoint argue that human beings are not programmed to develop in a specific way because we have free will, can make lifestyle choices and are influenced by a complex range of psychological, social, geographic and economic factors.

See also -Environmental factors; Genetic factors; Biological factors

textbook
training

Osteoarthritis

Osteoarthritis is a long-term condition that causes a person's joints to become stiff and painful.

Most joints in the body can be affected by osteoarthritis but it usually affects a person's hips, knees or hand joints. The severity of symptoms varies considerably between people. In some cases, a person's symptoms come and go and are mild whilst in others they are continuous and severe enough to affect their ability to look after themselves and carry out everyday living tasks. Pain and stiffness in the joints are the main symptoms of osteoarthritis. Other symptoms include:

- tender or sore joints, especially after a period of inactivity
- a grating sound or sensation in the affected joints
- joints appearing larger and more 'knobbly' than usual
- loss of muscle bulk and weakness
- restricted movement in the affected joints.

The precise causes of osteoarthritis are unknown. Factors that seem linked to osteoarthritis include:

- Wear and tear of the joints, leading to loss or damage to the cartilage that protects the bones and allows them to move freely,
- joint injuries and over-use of a joint before the injury has fully healed,
- increasing age
- a family history of osteoarthritis
- obesity

**textbook
training**

Maintaining a healthy weight (or losing weight if obese / overweight) and taking regular exercise that strengths muscles and joints, improves fitness and reduces stress can all help to prevent and reduce osteoarthritis symptoms. There is currently no cure for the condition. People with severe symptoms that are disabling may also be prescribed pain relief medication and have regular physiotherapy to help manage the pain and stiffness they experience.

See also –Ageing process; Biological factors; Environmental factors; Genetic factors

Oestrogen

Oestrogen is a group of steroid hormones, secreted largely by the ovaries and placenta, that promote secondary sexual development in females and which stimulates ovulation.

Males and females secrete both oestrogen and testosterone as a normal part of their physical functioning. However, males generally secrete more testosterone than females and females generally secrete more oestrogen than males. These differences in levels of hormone secretion largely account for differences in physical growth and development during adolescence. At the end of puberty, hormonal activity slows down and the rate of physical change reduces dramatically as a result.

Oestrogen also plays an important part in regulating menstruation and in pregnancy in adult women. For example, oestrogen hormones cause the lining of the womb to thicken during the menstrual cycle. If a pregnancy occurs, oestrogen is also created by the placenta to enable the woman's body to maintain the pregnancy. Following birth, oestrogen hormones suppress the menstrual cycle of the woman preventing ovulation from occurring. Healthcare practitioners suggest that this is to ensure that a breastfeeding mother is able to fully nourish her baby at a time when ovulation is prevented from occurring.

In more general health terms, oestrogen is also thought to play a part in maintaining healthy bones, promoting skin health and regulating cholesterol. The decline in a woman's oestrogen production during middle adulthood leads to menopause and can result in reduced bone density (osteoporosis), fatigue and hot flushes.

See also – Hormones; Puberty; Adolescence; Human growth; Human development; Maturity; Biological factors; Perimenopause; Menopause

textbook training

Parenting style

The concept of parenting style refers to the approach parents take in the way they bring up their children. This includes the psychological, relationship and communication strategies a parent habitually uses as part of their child-rearing.

During childhood a balance needs to be achieved between the child's emerging skills and need for autonomy and the parents need to protect the child / control the child's behaviour. A child's parents have a major role to play in socialising the child. Their approach to the way in which the child is brought up, or parented, is seen as having a major effect on the child's ongoing social and personality development. Psychologists have identified four categories of 'parenting style'.

Figure 22 – Different parenting styles

Parenting style	What happens?	Consequences
Authoritative	Involves parents combining control with acceptance and child-centred involvement. Their control of and demands on the child to behave in particular ways is combined with warmth, nurturance and two-way communication. Authoritative parents take their children's opinions and feelings into account and give explanations and reasons for punishing them where this occurs.	The children of authoritative parents tend to be friendly, independent, self-assertive and co-operative with their parents. They seem to grow up enjoying life and have a strong motivation to succeed.

textbook training

Parenting style	What happens?	Consequences
Authoritarian	Involves parents also trying to control and assert their power over their children. In contrast to authoritative parenting this happens without the parents communicating warmth and nurturance to their children. Authoritarian parents attempt to set absolute standards, make obedience an important issue, and place a high regard on respect for authority, work, tradition and orderliness.	The consequences of authoritarian parenting tends to be that children are moderately competent and responsible but are also socially withdrawn and lack spontaneity. Girls can be more dependent on their parents and to lack achievement motivation. Boys tend to be more aggressive than usual. There is also a link between low self-esteem and authoritarian parenting.
Indulgent	Indulgent parents adopt a parenting style that is accepting, responsive and child-centred. They tend to place few demands on their children and exercise little control over their behaviour.	Children who have had indulgent parents tend to show more happiness and vitality than other children but lack social assurance, self-reliance and impulse control.

textbook
training

Parenting style	What happens?	Consequences
Neglectful	Neglectful parents are very parent-centred individuals who are concerned with their own interests and are relatively uninvolved with the concerns and activities of their children compared to other type of parent. Neglectful parents also have fewer conversations with their children, are less aware of their school progress or 'social life' and do not take their children's opinions into account when making decisions.	The children of neglectful parents tend to be moody, impulsive and aggressive. They are more likely to develop delinquent behaviour.

Critics of 'parenting style' models like the one above argue that parents are not always, or even at any point in time, one or other 'type' of parent. They may use more than one parenting style and if there are two parents in a family they may use different parenting styles. Critics of the concept of parenting style also suggest that whilst it may describe the emotional climate of parent-child relationships, what really matters are parenting *practices*- that is, what parents actually do. Some parents are much more involved with their children in a practical, everyday way than others, for example. Parental practices such as being supportive, monitoring behaviour and maintaining firm boundaries are linked to better educational attainment, fewer behaviour problems and better mental health in children.

See also – Attachment; Self -concept; Self-esteem; Infancy; Social development; Emotional development

Peer pressure

Peer pressure is the influence that a person's peer group can exert over their attitudes, values or behaviour.

Friends approximately the same age as you and other people with whom you share similarities, important connections or whom you identify with are usually described as members of your peer group. Gender, ethnicity and leisure interests could therefore form the basis of non-age related peer groups. When a person identifies with and wishes to belong to a peer group, they are most susceptible to peer pressure.

Peer groups are an important influence on human development during childhood and adolescence. Emotional and social development during adolescence is closely linked to relationships with same- and opposite-sex friends, for example. An adolescent's attitudes and values, ways of behaving and sense of self-worth is significantly affected by these friendships and by peer group expectations. This is largely because adolescence involves a search for a sense of personal 'identity'.

Taking cues from and being like friends are strategies that many teenagers use as they try to achieve this important sense of 'self'. This doesn't mean to say that friendships in other life stages (childhood, adulthood or old age) don't influence personal development.

They do, but not usually in such a powerful, formative way. Friendships are very important in children's social and emotional development and play a vital role in supporting and sustaining an adult's sense of identity, belonging and sense of self-esteem.

However, peer groups, and conformity to the values, taste, styles and behaviours of peers, is most pronounced during adolescence.

Peer pressure is most associated with risk-taking behaviour. An adolescent is more likely to engage in anti-social and risk-taking behaviour if the peer group they are closely involved with is also risk-taking. However, peer pressure can also promote more positive behaviour and motivate adolescents to 'fit in' with friends who are motivated to achieve high academic standards, develop sporting, musical or artistic skills or live in a way that reflects the environmental, political or other social values of their peers.

Figure 23 – Resisting peer pressure can make you feel like the odd one out.

> **See also** – Friendships; Adolescence; Social development; Bullying; Self-concept; Self-esteem; Self-image

textbook
training

Perimenopause

The perimenopause is the period in a woman's life leading up to her menopause.

The perimenopause can last between 4 and 8 years but may be shorter or longer. There is no precise way of predicting when perimenopause will start or end and many women are unaware that their perimenopause has begun until they have almost reached then end of the process. Physiological changes characteristics of menopause are experienced during the perimenopause. For example, an increase in oestrogen levels is responsible during this transition period for symptoms such as hot flushes, night sweats, sleeping difficulties and vaginal dryness. The risk of heart disease and osteoporosis is also increased as a result of the physiological changes that occur during the perimenopause period.

Figure 24 – Perimenopause is linked to a range of developmental changes that affect women in middle adulthood.

See also – Adulthood; Physical development; Hormones; Oestrogen; Biological factors

Phenylketonuria (PKU)

Phenylketonuria is an inherited metabolic condition that approximately 1 in 10 000 babies are born with. A baby with PKU has an impaired ability to metabolise the amino acid phenylalanine.

Phenylalanine is a necessary, natural part of the human diet. However, if a person has too much phenylalanine from protein-rich foods (meat, fish, eggs, milk) or from eating foods containing the artificial sweetener aspartame (yoghurts, ice creams, sweets) they can be poisoned. Normally, a naturally produced enzyme, phenylalanine hydroxylase (PAH), breaks down any excess phenylalanine from food in the human body. However, people with PKU have little or no effective PAH and risk a toxic build-up of phenylalanine in their blood and brain. This can impair brain development and function and lead to intellectual disabilities, epileptic seizures and other behavioural and medical problems.

PKU is easily identified through a heel-prick blood test given to babies shortly after birth. Regular blood tests, a controlled, low-protein diet and amino acid supplements are the main treatments for PKU in childhood. A person who has this condition may stay on a low protein diet and take supplements for the rest of their life, though this isn't always necessary in adulthood. People who have regular blood tests and who stick to a low-protein diet with amino acid supplements are likely to experience normal mental development and a normal lifespan.

See also – Genetic factors; Learning disabilities; Intellectual development; Infancy

textbook
training

Physical Development

Physical growth and development can be directly observed over relatively short periods of time. This is particularly the case in the early years of life and during adolescence when physical changes are very noticeable and occur rapidly. Physical change during adulthood and old age involves less *growth* but should not be thought of as simply involving physical decline. The key features of physical growth and development in each life stage are described below.

Infancy is probably the most action-packed phase of growth and development in the human life course. The rapid pace of physical growth and development that began at conception and which continued through nine months of foetal development, shows little sign of slowing down when a baby is born. Physical change during the first three years of life transforms an infant's appearance. Infants grow taller and generally gain weight very quickly. During the first eighteen months of life, an infant's body weight will triple.

An infant's physical growth and development follows a predictable pattern. Physical change occurs from the head downwards (cephalocaudal) and from the middle of the body outwards (proximodistal). An infant will first develop gross **motor skills –** basic, unsophisticated movement of their limbs, trunk and head – that enable them to hold their head up without support, to hold on to people and large objects and later to crawl about.

The physical foundations of infant development
The physical growth and changes that occur in early infancy provide an essential foundation for various forms of growth and development that occur later in the human life course. These changes include:

- ossification or hardening of the baby's soft bones - this allows for independent movement and makes the infant more physically robust
- brain growth – this enables the infant to develop language and thinking skills which, in turn, give the child relationship building and social skills

In the later stages of infancy, children begin to develop fine motor skills. These are more sophisticated and finely controlled forms of movement. They enable a child to eat with cutlery, do up zips and buttons and tie their shoe laces, for example. Between the ages of 2 and 3 years, most infants will be able to run quite easily, climb onto and get off

Physical growth and development in early childhood (3-8 years)
During childhood, individuals gradually move from being physically dependent, immobile infants, to being more physically capable and competent children. The pace of physical change experienced by the human body is slower during childhood than it was in infancy. On average, during each year of childhood a child will:

- grow between 5 and 7.5 centimetres (2-3 inches)
- gain about 2.7 kilograms (6 pounds) in weight

At the same time, motor development is extended and consolidated. Developing children:

- become increasingly physically capable, skilled and robust
- can move easily and skilfully
- develop and use hand / eye co-ordination effectively

Improvements in motor skills during later childhood allow the child to move and complete tasks faster, and with better co-ordination, than they were able to a few years earlier. Girls tend to have more body fat and less muscle tissue than boys at this age but have very similar abilities in terms of speed and strength. Hormonal changes begin in to occur towards the end of this stage but their effects can't really be seen until a few years later.

During later childhood (6 to 8) there is a continuing pattern of gradual, steady physical growth and development. Qualitative improvements in motor skills allow the child to move and complete tasks faster, and with better co-ordination, than they were able to in the previous phase. Girls tend to have more body fat and less muscle tissue than boys at this age but have very similar abilities in terms of speed and strength. Hormonal changes begin in to occur towards the end of this stage but their effects are not really evident until a few years later.

Physical growth and development in adolescence (9-18 years)
Adolescence is a period of rapid, major physical growth and development. This is in contrast to the relative lack, and slow pace, of physical change in late childhood. Puberty is the term used to describe the period in adolescence when physical changes to the human reproductive system leads to sexual maturity. As a result of puberty, boys can produce sperm and girls can produce eggs that, when fertilised by sperm, can result in a pregnancy and birth of a baby. Girls tend to begin puberty about two years earlier than boys of the same age.

The influence of hormones
The physical changes that occur during puberty are mainly the result of hormone activity. Hormones are the secretions of the endocrine glands. The body produces a number of hormones from several different endocrine glands.

textbook training

As a result of increased hormone production, physical growth and development occurs in the primary and secondary sexual characteristics of both males and females during adolescence.

Physical growth and development in early adulthood (19-45 years)
Physical maturity is reached in adulthood. This is the phase of the life course where most people are at their physical peak. As a young adult, a person is likely to have more muscle tissue, stronger bones, better eyesight, hearing and smell, greater oxygen capacity and a more efficient immune system than at any other point in their life.

Human fertility peaks, or is strongest, in early adulthood. An adult woman's fertility is strongest in her early 20's and the drops considerably after the age of 35. Male fertility also follows this pattern, with men in their 20's producing better quality, more fertile sperm than older men. Despite the pattern of gradual decline in fertility, many couples manage to conceive and produce children in the later stages of early adulthood.

The ageing process begins...
In the years leading up to adulthood, physical growth and development has occurred largely as a result of **maturation**. From early adulthood onwards, the **ageing process** takes over from maturation, affecting the way we change physically as well as our cognitive (intellectual) and psychological functioning. Examples of how the ageing process affects physical functioning are identified in the table below.

See also –Human development; Human growth; Infancy; Motor skills; Puberty; Maturity; Hormones; Perimenopause; Menopause; Ageing process; Biological factors

---

Piaget's model

Jean Piaget (1895 – 1980) was a Swiss psychologist who developed a cognitive theory of intellectual development that has been influential in areas of work such as early years care, special needs support and primary education.

Piaget's research, much of it based on detailed observation of his own and other children, led him to conclude that the development of intelligence proceeds in four successive psychological stages:

- During the *sensorimotor stage* (0-2 years) infants experience the outside environment mainly through their senses and motor (physical) activity. The infant begins life with innate biological reflexes, some of which are modified through trial and error. The infant begins to 'think' about her world, initially in terms of what she can actually see, but, at eight, nine or ten months, she starts looking for hidden objects

- The *pre-operational stage* (2-7 years) is characterised by the gradual development of language and the ability to think in 'symbols'. For example, the word 'ball' (a symbol) is understood to represent a real ball that isn't in view.

- The *concrete operational stage* (7-11) marks the beginning of operational (that is, logical) thinking that can be applied to concrete problems, as long as they're related to personal experience. A child in this period can, for example, rank play objects like dolls in order of size, but needs to see and handle them in order to do this

textbook
training

- The *formal operational stage* (11 years and older) is a more advanced thinking period in which the child, and later the adult, gradually progresses from concrete to abstract problem-solving. People at this stage can still think concretely, but can also use quite complex mathematical and linguistic concepts

According to Piaget, all children proceed through these four learning stages one after the other. Even though the rates do differ somewhat (for example, a ten-year-old might be at the formal operations stage), Piaget argued that the *sequence* of development is the same for all children.

In Piaget's model, ways of thinking belonging to earlier stages become incorporated into the stages that follow, so that one builds upon the other. Because Piaget's theory is concerned with how humans construct and re-construct their knowledge and understanding of the world through different developmental stages, he's called a constructivist and his theory often goes by the name of constructivism.

In some cases, of course, earlier forms of reasoning, such as 'Father Christmas gives us presents', is replaced, rather than built on, by more logical forms. These ways of thinking, or *schemes*, are inner representations of outer realities. They're what children and all humans construct in their minds in order to understand what's going on around them. Constructions aren't, of course, exact copies of our outside world, just estimates.

Nor are they simply 'right' or 'wrong'. For example, "Father Christmas gives me presents", is an appropriate construction for a young child. It 'explains' the presents in the stocking from the child's point of view. It's 'right', given her level of development.

But we'd expect a more 'advanced' explanation from an older child: "Mum and Dad put them there" (Sorry, if you didn't realise).

What causes a child's development to move from one stage to another, from simple to more elaborate constructions of the world? Piaget attributes these transitions to:

- *maturation* (for example, the development of a brain and body that enables a child to walk and thereby explore its world more fully)
- physical experience (for example, experimenting with objects, which promotes problem-solving)
- *social transmission* (for example, playing with adults and, in the process, learning a language)
- *equilibration*. This refers to the process of regaining intellectual balance once, for example, one finds out that 'Father Christmas' doesn't exist...

This last factor, *equilibration*, is particularly important in the learning process, and therefore deserves a bit more attention. All living things are born with a tendency to adapt to their environment. In humans, adaptation often involves learning new things. For example, a child might learn to push a door open by copying its parents' actions. It *assimilates* (takes in) what a parent does, and then does the same, using the assimilated knowledge that has now becomes a *scheme* (a construction).But, if the child encounters a door that opens by sliding, she's perplexed. The existing scheme can deal with doors that open when pushed but not with doors that require sliding. A state of *disequilibrium* exists. To open the sliding door, the child will have to *accommodate* (adjust) to the new environment.

She might work out the solution by chance or trial and error or perhaps a parent will teach her how to slide the door open.Either way, once she's able to open the sliding door by herself, she will have *assimilated* a new *scheme*, in which case *accommodation* will have occurred. In Piaget's model *accommodation* means learning. Through the process of accommodation (that is, learning), either the individual's existing scheme is modified or a new one emerges.

Piaget's (constructivist) cognitive theory today

Although recent research has shown that Piaget underestimated the intelligence of children and overestimated the intelligence of adults, educational practice is still influenced by his model of cognitive development. A number of important principles derive from Piaget's work. These include:

- When the gap between what a child understands and what a teacher expects of them is too wide, a child won't learn.
- The child's thinking must be sufficiently developed before learning can take place
- When the gap between what a child understands and what's being taught is slightly greater than the level of understanding, a child is likely to learn

Getting the match right between the complexity of the subject matter and what the child understands and is able, with a bit of effort, to understand is crucial. A good way of creating a realistic and achievable 'learning dilemma' is to set a task that, with perhaps a little adult guidance, a child will 'discover' the solution to on her own.

See also – Cognitive approach; Infancy; Intellectual development; Conservation

textbook
training

Play

Play is generally thought of as non-serious activity that people engage in for fun, enjoyment or recreation. In a human development context, play is seen as an important way through which infants and children in particular develop a range of physical, intellectual, social and emotional abilities and skills.

Children who attend pre-school childcare and early years learning settings such as playgroups, nurseries, crèches, kindergartens and childminders, participate in lots of play activities. This is because play provides a wide range of learning opportunities for pre-school children. Learning to play with other children by sharing toys, taking turns and co-operating provides some early social development opportunities, for example. A child's social skills develop and improve as they learn to communicate and spend time with other children taking part in different types of play activity. These include:

Solitary or solo play
The first stage of play involves a child playing alone. Babies and young children can be very contented playing on their own and frequently show no interest in wanting to play with others. This gradually changes as the child becomes more aware of and able to communicate with other children.

Parallel play
This type of play involves a child playing alongside – but not with – another child. Children move from solitary/solo play to parallel play as they build up their self-confidence and become more familiar with other children.

textbook
training

Looking–on play

This involves a child watching other children playing, often from the edge of a group of children or across a playground. The child shows interest in the activities of other children by looking-on but isn't ready or confident enough to join in.

Joining–in play

This occurs where a child is motivated and confident enough to join in play activities with another child. They may not be deliberately co-operating or sharing but will be happy to participate in the same type of play activity.

Co–operative play

This is the stage of play where children actually co-operate with each other, playing together in a deliberate way. Co-operative play can occur between a couple of children who communicate and share an activity together or within a larger group of children.

Learning through play

Play is a natural, enjoyable way for children to learn. Children can use play to investigate and explore the world around them, develop their physical, intellectual and social skills and as a way of expressing their imagination and emotions. For example, physical play is a way of getting and keeping a child's developing body in good shape, and provides children with an outlet for their physical energy and ways of testing out the physical skills and abilities they develop. By contrast, creative play enables a child to develop and use intellectual and physical – especially fine motor – skills as it usually involves activities that are both mentally absorbing and 'hands on'. 'Let's pretend' games and other imaginative play activities become a feature of children's play from about the age of 2.

textbook
training

Dressing up tends to be a very popular activity with both boys and girls. Role-play games in which children pretend to be 'mum', 'dad', their teacher or another significant adult, acting out stories or pretending to be characters from their favourite cartoons are also ways children explore, develop and express emotions in a safe, non-threatening way.

Social play involves co-operation with other children (and sometimes adults). It enables children to learn how to tolerate others, and to share and work with them. Children can learn to understand the roles, needs and perspectives of others through social play. Playing closely and co-operatively with other children also requires the child to control their own behaviour and express their emotions in a socially acceptable way.

Figure 25 – Children's play can promote development in a number of different ways.

> **See also** – Infancy; Piaget's model; Egocentrism; Social development; Emotional development; Attachment; Friendships; Intellectual development; Conservation

textbook training

Pollution

Pollution occurs when the natural environment is contaminated with harmful substances.

Physical growth and development can be directly affected by the presence of pollution in the atmosphere. Levels of air pollution in the United Kingdom have changed very little since the early 1980's. As a result, air pollution continues to contribute to the higher levels of respiratory problems (including asthmatic symptoms and bronchitis) that are prevalent in urban areas of the United Kingdom. Carbon monoxide and other harmful gas emissions from vehicles, ships and factories can be particularly damaging to a person's respiratory system. Babies and children can have their growth potential restricted, though people at all stages of life can have their physical health damaged by the effects of poor air quality. Noise pollution from vehicles, aircraft and busy crowded environments can also damage a person's hearing and their psychological wellbeing. Unwanted noise is also associated with high stress levels, sleep disturbances and high blood pressure. Noise pollution is worst in built-up, urban environments.

See also – Environmental factors

textbook
training

Psychological change

Psychological change refers to changes that occur in a person's mental abilities, ways of thinking and cognitive capacities.

Psychological change can occur as a result of social, emotional and intellectual development during the human life span. For example, psychological change occurs as an individual develops their cognitive and language abilities as they move through infancy, childhood and adolescence. Similarly, Piaget argued that adolescents and adults experience significant psychological change as they develop abstract thinking abilities. Psychological change can also result from the experience of significant life events that trigger a shift in a person's self-image and broader self-concept. For example, a person may experience a significant shift in their self-concept when they get married, establish a long-term relationship or become a parent. Where an individual experience a form of mental distress, from bereavement perhaps, their experience of this and any subsequent therapeutic treatment and support they receive may also trigger psychological change as they adapt to and accommodate the impact of the life event on their sense of self.

See also – Attachment; Emotional development; Life events; Chomsky's theory; Cognitive development; Intellectual development; Piaget's theory; Self-image; Stress-diathesis model; Bandura's theory.

textbook
training

Puberty

Puberty is the term used to describe the period in adolescence when physical changes to the human reproductive system leads to sexual maturity.

As a result of puberty, boys can produce sperm and girls can produce eggs that, when fertilised by sperm, can result in a pregnancy and birth of a baby. Girls tend to begin puberty about two years earlier than boys of the same age. The growth spurt and physical changes that occur in puberty are caused by an increase in hormonal activity. Hormones are chemical secretions that pass directly into the blood from the endocrine glands.

The thyroid gland and the pituitary gland are the two main glands that secrete growth and development hormones. The pituitary gland controls the production of hormones that affect growth and development. The pituitary gland is located at the base of the brain and is only the size of a pea. The thyroid gland is located in the neck. It influences our general growth rate, bone and muscle development and the functioning of our reproductive organs.

During puberty the testes in boys produce the hormone testosterone and the ovaries in girls produce oestrogen and progesterone. These hormones control the development and function of the reproductive organs. During puberty, boys and girls develop the secondary sexual characteristics that enable them to produce children and which give them their adult body shape.

Physical changes in puberty

Physical changes in boys	Physical changes in girls
Grow taller and heavier	Grow taller and heavier
Grow pubic, facial and underarm hair	Menstruation (periods) start
Penis and testes grow larger	Develop breasts
Shoulders and chest broaden and muscles develop	Hips broaden and shape changes
Voice 'breaks' or deepens	Grow pubic and underarm hair

See also – **Hormones;** Adolescence; Human growth; Human development; Maturity; Self-concept; Self-image; Self-esteem

Self-concept

This refers to the combination of self-image and self-esteem that together produce a sense of personal identity.

A child's sense of 'self' – who they are – is relatively simple and clear. In early childhood children don't tend to reflect and make judgements about their overall 'self-worth' and have a limited 'self-image'. They tend to think about and describe who they are in terms of their visible, physical characteristics and can say how good they think they are at familiar physical, intellectual and social tasks. For example, a child might say "I'm no good at counting but I am good at running". This starts to change in later childhood but becomes more evident as a person enters and progresses through adolescence. Cognitive and emotional development during adolescence put a person's sense of 'self' (who they are and who they wish to be) .

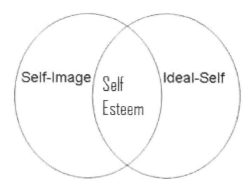

Figure 26 – Self-concept consists of a number of different elements.

Children begin to develop a more sophisticated sense of self as they enter adolescence and experience cognitive and emotional developments. In particular, adolescents gradually become more self-aware and become more sensitive to the thoughts and beliefs of others. Many adolescents also develop abstract thinking abilities, enabling them to consider how they could develop in order to achieve their 'ideal self (who they want to be). This might be informed by values and beliefs and can be influenced by the thoughts, opinions and ways in which others react or relate to them. By the end of this life stage a child will tend to have an awareness of her own internal qualities, beliefs and personality traits. She will now be able to make global judgements about her self-worth and self-esteem.

See also – Attachment; Adolescence; Emotional development; Social development; Friendships; Sibling rivalry; Psychological change

Self-esteem

Self-esteem refers to a person's sense of their self-worth.

A person's self-esteem consists of beliefs about themselves ('I am kind', 'I am useless', 'I am unlovable', 'I am beautiful') as well emotions the person feels about themselves (pride, shame, sadness, happiness). In essence, self-esteem is a judgement that expresses what we think and feel about our 'self'.

Psychologists generally see self-esteem as a core, enduring feature of an individual's personality and a factor that influences motivation and attainment in a person's education, work and personal life. An individual with positive or high self-esteem is, for example, thought to be more likely to be happy, achieve well and feel fulfilled in their personal life and relationships. By contrast, a person with low self-esteem is thought to be more likely to be self-critical, pessimistic and envious of others. Self-esteem plays an important part in humanistic psychology.

See also – Self-concept; Self-image; Psychological change; Bullying; Adolescence; Social development; Emotional development; Friendships; Peer pressure

Self-harm

The concept of self-harm refers to any form of deliberate self-injury that is intentional but not suicidal.

Skin-cutting and self-poisoning are the most common forms of self-harm. Other less common forms include hair-pulling (trichotillomania), opening up cuts and wounds to prevent healing (dermatillomania), burning, scratching or hitting body parts and swallowing objects or toxic substances. There is usually a deliberate attempt to cause tissue damage in any form of self-harm. Adolescents and young adults are most likely to self-harm but self-harm does occur in all age groups.

Self-harming behaviour can be life-threatening and may have unintentionally fatal consequences. Some people do self-harm without having a diagnosed mental health problem. However, self-harm may also be a symptom of other conditions such as depression, eating disorder, post-traumatic stress, anxiety disorder or borderline personality disorder.

People give a variety of reasons for self-harming. For example, for some people use self-harm as a way of coping with extreme stress, intense anxiety, depression, feelings of failure or a deep sense of self-loathing and low self-esteem. A person's self-harming behaviour may be linked to traumatic events that have happened to them – such as child abuse, sexual assault or traumatic loss – or may be linked to ongoing patterns of dysfunctional or destructive behaviour like perfectionism, addiction or self-image problems.

People who present with self-harm injuries at Accident and Emergency departments have often consumed excessive amounts of alcohol prior to self-harming.

There are a number of different forms of treatment and support for self-harm, including:

- drug treatments, especially if self-harm is linked to anxiety or depression
- teaching avoidance techniques that aim to occupy the person with other activities when they are stressed and likely to self-harm
- harm-minimisation approaches, such as needle exchanges for heroin addicts, that aim to reduce the risk involved in some self-harming behaviours
- Cognitive behavioural therapy that challenges dysfunctional thinking and destructive patterns of behaviour and equips the person with alternative ways of thinking and behaving.
- Relaxation / mindfulness techniques that aim to reduce underlying tensions and help the person to avoid stress and situations that may trigger their self-harming behaviour.

See also – Self-concept; Self-esteem; Bullying; Stress-diathesis model

textbook
training

Self-image

A person's self-image is the generally stable mental picture they have of themselves – how they see, and believe others see, themselves as a person.

The components of self-image include objective information about physique and physical characteristics (height / weight, hair and eye colour, skin tone etc). Perhaps more importantly though, it also includes subjective information about what the person feels about themselves and how they think others judge and feel about them.

Self-image is important because it affects self-esteem, emotions and a person's broader mental health. This, in turn impacts on how a person relates to (or feels able to make relationships with) others. A negative self-image may develop if a person experiences criticism, particularly from an authority figure during childhood. This can damage the view the person has of themselves as a person and reduce their self-esteem. Similarly, people who set very high, perhaps unattainable, standards for themselves are prone to negative self-image as they frequently fail to achieve their self-defined standards of success. Other social standards relating to physical appearance, beauty and desirable personality characteristics may also predispose some people to negative self-image because they aspire to standards or qualities they can never achieve.

See also –Self-concept; Self-esteem; Social development; Emotional development

Sibling rivalry

This term is used to refer to competition, and sometimes hostility, between siblings (brothers / sisters) in a family.

Sibling rivalry can begin in infancy and continue throughout each person's life. During childhood and adolescence, siblings are sensitive to the way they are treated by parents, particularly in comparison to their siblings. Competition, resentment and hostility may build -up and be expressed if one or more siblings believe they are treated less favourably than the other(s) or if they suspect a sibling of seeking preferential treatment. Siblings are better able to deal with emotional, psychological or intellectual challenges from siblings than they were earlier in life because they are more likely to be emotionally mature and will spend less time with each other. The older siblings get, the less intense any rivalry tends to be.

Parents can minimise and even prevent sibling rivalry in infancy and early childhood by:

- avoiding any kind of favouritism – ensuring fair and equal treatment
- involving existing children in the care of the new baby
- being affectionate and giving time to each child
- talking about and explaining what sibling relationships should involve.

See also – Parenting style; Friendships; Social development; Emotional development; Family dysfunction

Social development

Social development involves the emergence and improvement of communication skills and relationships with other people.

The way individuals develop social relationships, interact and communicate with others is strongly influenced by the society and culture in which they grow up and develop. A person's social relationships and their ability to communicate effectively with others will have a significant impact on how they feel about themselves and others and how they are able to express and deal with their feelings.

Childhood social development

Social development during childhood builds on the foundations established during infancy. During childhood children try to form new relationships with new people in new situations – such as with teachers at school and with other children who become their friends. Significant features of social development that occur during childhood include:

- the development of further communication and relationship building skills
- an increase in the number and variety of relationships with people outside of the family
- a greater degree of independence from parents
- an improvement in the ability to use social and language skills to manage personal relationships with others

textbook
training

Children gradually develop greater awareness of who they are and how they are similar to and different from others. A child can usually identify their own sex (boy or girl) by the age of two. However, it is not until they reach five or six years of age that most children realise that this feature of their identity is fixed! This concept is known as *gender constancy*. It forms an important part of a child's developing sense of 'self'.

Relationships with friends become increasingly important during childhood. In fact, by the middle of childhood many children prefer to spend time with their peers rather than their parents and can become quite embarrassed by parental attention when their friends are around! Childhood friendships tend to be very sex-segregated with boys preferring to make friends with other boys and girls establishing friendships with other girls.

Children's ideas about 'self'
A child's sense of 'self' – who they are – is relatively simple and clear. In early childhood children don't tend to reflect and make judgements about their overall 'self-worth'. Instead they tend to think about and describe who they are in terms of their visible characteristics and can say how good they think they are at familiar physical, intellectual and social tasks. For example, a child might say "I'm no good at counting but I am good at running". Children develop a clearer self-concept as they progress through childhood. By the end of this life stage a child will tend to have an awareness of her own internal qualities, beliefs and personality traits. She will now be able to make global judgements about her self-worth and self-esteem.

Adolescent social development

Adolescence is often seen as an emotionally difficult and 'stormy' life stage. Teenagers' turbulent hormones are often blamed for their 'moodiness' and emotional sensitivity.

The significant physical changes that adolescents experience often trigger off concerns about 'being normal' and about self-image. Adolescents tend to need reassurance about their growth patterns and their sense of self. They may seek this from friends, parents, teachers, magazines and other media. The social and emotional consequences of physical maturation during adolescence show how these developmental processes are intertwined rather than separate. For example, early maturation can result in increased attention and extra responsibility, especially for boys. For girls, it can result in unwanted sexual attention, pressure and awkwardness. Alternatively, late maturation can damage self-confidence and self-esteem in some adolescents who feel that they are 'out of sync' with their peers and who may be teased or bullied as a result.

Friendships in adolescence

Relationships with friends play a very important role in social (and emotional) development during adolescence. Friendships are more stable and adolescents generally spend more time with their peers than they did during childhood. An adolescent's friendship group becomes a means of transition from family to independent, adult life. It is by using their increasing social opportunities and their ability to choose and make new relationship with peers that adolescents gradually separate from their parents.

textbook
training

Adult social development

People typically leave home to live independently of their family in early adulthood. Greater independence requires new relationships. Often young adults make new friendships through work and social life, focusing quite strongly on finding a partner and sustaining an intimate relationship.

New responsibilities and an extension of the person's social circle may also result from marriage or cohabitation. Much of adulthood is concerned with trying to find a balance between the competing demands of work, family and friends. Each of these types of relationship contribute to social development by giving the person a sense of connection and belonging to others.

New parenthood is also a feature of early adulthood. For most people it appears to be an experience that brings profound satisfaction, a greater sense of purpose and increased self-worth. It also introduces a number of role changes. Sex roles and spouse relationships tend to change when children arrive. The birth of children appears to result in a drop in partners' relationship satisfaction and an increase in 'role strain' because the roles of partner and spouse are at least partly incompatible.

The roles of partner, parent and worker that are a feature of adulthood change as an individual progress' through this life stage. Children leaving home usually affect the role of parent. Work tends to be less demanding and there are usually fewer potential promotion opportunities by middle age.

Relationships, especially partnerships, are likely to be given more time and assume a new significance. Whilst individual experiences clearly vary this tends to be the optimum time of life for many people.

textbook
training

Partnership satisfaction tends to rise in mid-life, possibly due to the reduction in role strain that also occurs. Effectively partners have more time to spend together in mid-adulthood. Also poor marriages tend to have ended by this point.

Social development in later adulthood

Later adulthood is a time when considerable changes in roles and relationships are experienced. The role of worker is largely lost as people retire. The role of spouse is lost when a partner dies. The role of son or daughter is lost when parents die. The roles that remain are less complex and usually involve fewer duties.

Partner relationships in later life tend to be based on loyalty, familiarity and mutual investment in the relationship. Partners tend to spend more time with each other. Older women expect to be widowed and to live on their own for a time, older men don't. Older people tend to see their children regularly for purposes of practical help and emotional support. Continuity and adaptation are the themes of later adulthood relationships. Bee (1995) referred to the creation of a 'convoy' of relationships throughout life. This is 'a protective layer of family and friends who surround us and help us to deal with life's challenges'. This 'convoy' seems to be relatively stable over time once established. People tend to choose friends who have similar social and psychological characteristics and who are at the same life-stage.

See also – Self-concept; Self-image; Infancy; Play; Emotional development; Friendships; Peer pressure; Adolescence

Reference
H. Bee (1995), *The Developing Child*, Harlow, Longman.

textbook
training

Social disengagement theory

Cumming and Henry (1961) proposed disengagement theory as a way of explaining behaviour and development in old age. They suggested that when people reached their sixties they began to 'disengage' from active roles in society for a variety of reasons. For example, disengagement could happen because of:

- ill-health
- retirement from work
- loss of friendships and social support (illness and death of partners, friends and relatives)
- lack of access to travel facilities
- inability to use communication technology (email, internet, ICT systems)

Cumming and Henry (1961) argued that disengagement in old age occurs voluntarily and with the approval of the younger generation because it frees up employment opportunities. This, they suggest, is a normal and appropriate response that has benefits for society and for older people.

See also – Ageing process; Activity theory

Reference
Cumming, E.and Henry, W.E. (1961) *Growing Old*, New York, Basic Books

Social factors

Social factors are the features of a society or the ways in which people live, such as religious or other beliefs, relationships, family and culture that have an impact on health and development experiences.

Social factors is a broad term that can include 'macro' social concepts such as social class and culture that affect the way in which society as a whole is organised and structured. At a population level, there are links between a person's social class, gender, ethnicity and their pattern of health and illness experience, for example. At a more 'micro' social level, experiences of bullying, discrimination and family dysfunction have a more direct, personal impact on an individual's health, wellbeing and development. All of these examples are linked by the fact that they are features of the way society is organised or operates at a whole society, group or individual level.

See also – Bullying; culture; discrimination; family dysfunction;

textbook
training

Stress-diathesis model

This focuses on the connection between stress and a person's vulnerability (diathesis) to certain conditions. The stress-diathesis model is used to explain why some people develop certain diseases and illness conditions and others don't despite their apparently similar behaviour and lifestyles. The answer is in the link between stress and diathesis (vulnerability).

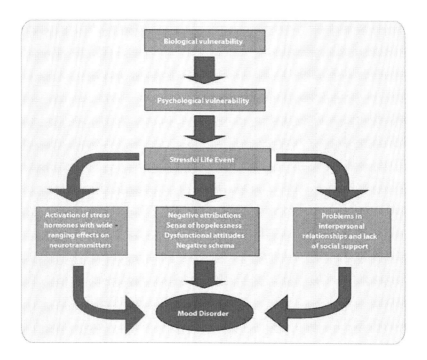

Figure 27 – An example of the stress-diathesis model

That is, people who have a pre-existing vulnerability to a condition such as mood disorder like depression (because of family history, for example), are more likely to develop that condition if exposed to particular stressors that trigger or exacerbate the condition.

In this case, a person's family history of depression suggests that they have inherited genes that predispose them to (but by themselves don't cause) this condition. If they then expose themselves to factors that trigger depression, they run a high risk of developing it. However, a person without a family history of depression is less vulnerable to developing it, even if they are exposed to depression triggers through stressful life events.

The stress-diathesis model helps to explain why:

- some people are more likely to develop certain conditions than other people (diathesis / 'vulnerability)

- some people with predisposing vulnerabilities develop a condition they are at greater risk of when others with the same predisposing vulnerabilities do not (exposure to stressors).

See also – Life events; Genetic factors; Environmental factors; Economic factors; Social factors; Nature-Nurture debate; Holmes and Rahe rating scale

---

30265680R00074

Printed in Great Britain
by Amazon